i can't believe i'm Knitting CABLES

You've always admired those talented knitters who can pick up their needles and create dazzling designs like Aran cardigans. Now there's no reason why you can't count yourself among them!

These easy-to-follow instructions will have you showing off your own knitted cables in no time. We start with the basics and add a new concept or technique until you've finished your first easy project. After that, you can create the remaining 13 cabled items that range from simple to simply stunning. Are you still thinking that cables are too intricate? With these step-by-step directions, the whole process is demystified, so you can indulge your creative spirit with the rich textures of cables. And there's even more assistance online—visit www.leisurearts.com and click on ***Webcasts*** to find the ***I Can't Believe I'm Knitting Cables*** live podcast.

You? Knitting cables? Yes, you can believe it after all!

LEISURE ARTS, INC.
Little Rock, Arkansas

ADDING MOTION WITH CABLES, TWISTS, AND BOBBLES

They may look intimidating, but they're really not. Taken step-by-step, cables and twists can be a wonderful addition to your knitting repertoire. They use the same knits and purls that you know so well, except they are swinging elbows with their partners in a textured dance on your knit fabric.

You've seen them traveling across fisherman sweaters, but let's take a closer look.

Cable textures are usually showcased by working knit stitches on a background of Reverse Stockinette Stitch like the one in Photo A. A more subtle effect is achieved with a Stockinette Stitch background as in Photo B. Photo C shows the same cable on a seed stitch background.

And how are cables made?

They're achieved with a simple twisting, an exchange of positions. In the most common form of cables, half of the cable stitches are put on hold on a cable needle, either in the front or in the back of your work. You work the next half of the stitches from the left needle, then you work the "on-hold" stitches, either by slipping them back onto the left needle and working them or by working directly from the cable needle.

Cable needles come in three basic shapes—a bent J-shape, smooth or grooved straight doubled pointed, and a double pointed with a dip in the middle. Sizes are made thick for heavier yarns and thinner for all other yarns. In a pinch, plastic coffee stirrers, crochet hooks, stitch holders, chopsticks, or safety pins can be used.

Photo A

Photo B

Photo C

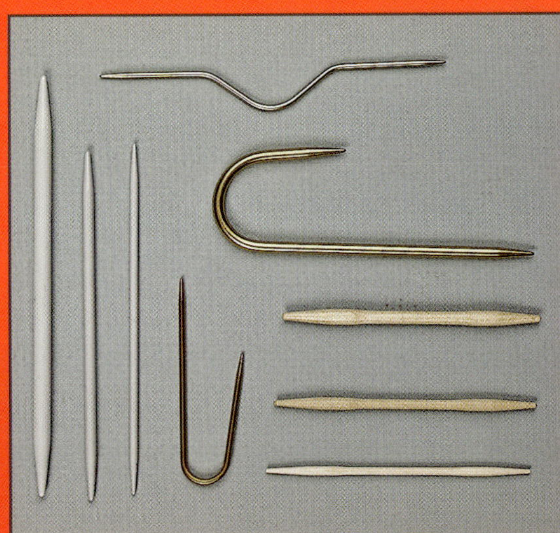

So, by a simple process of "hey, you stitches go over there and then you others come over here," a cable is formed.

Let's make a napkin ring while learning how to work simple front and back 4-stitch cables. You'll need about 10 yards (9 meters) of medium weight yarn, size 6 (4 mm) straight knitting needles, a cable needle, and a yarn needle.

We have a complete chart of this project so you can see how the stitches relate to one another as the cables progress. If you would like to try to work this pattern from the chart, start by casting on 10 sts. Use the key to identify the stitches and follow the chart from right to left on the right side rows and from left to right on the wrong side rows. Row numbers are placed on the side of the chart where you would begin each row—wrong side rows on the left edge and right side rows on the right edge. When you come to the cables, check that row in the written instructions to see the Figs. showing how to make the cables.

Cast on 10 sts.

Row 1 (Right side)**:** K2, P6, K2.

Row 2: Knit across.

Row 3: K2, P6, K2.

Row 4: K3, P4, K3.

Row 5: K2, P1, K4, P1, K2.

Row 6: K3, P4, K3.

Your first front cable will be worked with the center 4 stitches on the next row (see page 10 about front and back cables).

Instructions continued on page 4.

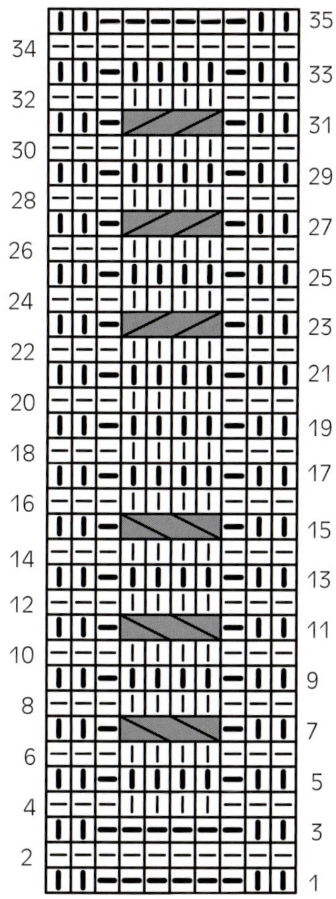

KEY

Purl wrong side

Knit right side

Knit wrong side

Purl right side

Front Cable

Back Cable

Row 7 (Cable row)**:**
Step 1: K2, P1, then slip next 2 stitches onto cable needle and hold them in the **front** of the work.

Step 2: Knit the next 2 stitches from the left needle.

Step 3: Knit the two stitches from the cable needle, making sure that they are worked in the order that they were slipped onto the cable needle (they really don't need any **extra** twists!).

Step 4: P1, K2 from left needle.

See how the last 2 cable stitches twist to the left? You will really start to see it after working the next one.

Rows 8-10: Repeat Rows 4-6.

Row 11 (Cable row)**:** Follow Steps 1-4 of Row 7 to complete another front cable ***(Photo A)***.

Rows 12-15: Repeat Rows 4-7.

At the end of Row 15, you'll have 3 front cables. Let's get some distance from the front cables before working the back cables.

Row 16: K3, P4, K3.

Row 17: K2, P1, K4, P1, K2.

Rows 18-22: Repeat Rows 16 and 17 twice, then repeat Row 16 once **more**.

Your first back cable will be worked in the center 4 stitches on the next row.

Step 1

Step 2

Step 3

Step 4

Photo A

Row 23 (Cable row)**:**
Step 1: K2, P1, slip next 2 stitches onto cable needle and hold them in the **back** of the work.

Step 2: Knit the next 2 stitches from the left needle.

Step 3: Knit the two stitches from the cable needle, making sure that they are worked in the order that they were slipped on the cable needle.

Step 4: P1, K2 from left needle.

See how the first 2 cable stitches twist to the right? You will really start to see it after working the next one.

Row 24: K3, P4, K3.

Row 25: K2, P1, K4, P1, K2.

Row 26: K3, P4, K3.

Row 27 (Cable row)**:** Follow Steps 1-4 of Row 23 to complete another back cable ***(Photo B)***.

Rows 28-33: Repeat Rows 24-27 once, then repeat Rows 24 and 25 once **more**.

Row 34: Knit across.

Row 35: K2, P6, K2.

Bind off all sts in **knit**, leaving a long end for sewing. Thread yarn needle with long end and sew cast on edge to bind off edge.

That was a lot of fun, wasn't it? Now, let's do the twist!

Is a twist just another cable?

A twist is a close relative to a cable. Right Twists and Left Twists are in fact simple little two stitch cables that can be worked without using a cable needle, either knitting in the front or the back of the second stitch on the left needle, then knitting the skipped first stitch (see Right Twist and Left Twist, page 75).

The major differences between twists and cables are that the stitches are perhaps not the same kind (all knits or all purls) or that odd numbers of stitches may be swapped. Of course, for every rule, there are the exceptions. There are twists with an even number of stitches like the ones in the Baby Pullover, page 24 and the Adult V-Neck Cardigan, page 44. Cables can also have an odd number of stitches as in the Large Pillow, page 65.

Let's work a swatch with a couple of twists, then add a popcorn and a bobble. Still using the same needles and yarn as you used for the napkin ring, cast on 11 sts.

Work in Stockinette Stitch for several rows, ending by working a knit row.

Row 1: K3, P2, K1, P2, K3.

Row 2 (Twist row)**:**
Let's work a Twist 3 Back first.

Purl the first 2 stitches.

Step 1: Slip the next purl stitch onto the cable needle and hold in back of the work.

Step 2: K2 from the left needle.

Step 3: P1 from the cable needle.

You have just made a Twist 3 Back. But, hold on, you have some stitches on your left needle to work a Twist 3 Front.

Purl the next stitch.

Step 4: Slip the next 2 knit stitches onto the cable needle and hold in front of work.

Step 5: P1 from the left needle.

Step 6: K2 from the cable needle.

Purl the last 2 stitches. You've made a back twist and a front twist on the same row *(Photo A)*.

Row 3: K2, P2, K3, P2, K2.

Row 4: P1, follow Steps 1-3 to make a back twist, P3, then follow Steps 4-6 to make a front twist, purl the last stitch.

Row 5: K1, P2, K5, P2, K1.

Let's reverse direction of the twists.

Row 6: P1, follow Steps 4-6 to make a front twist, P3, then follow Steps 1-3 to make a back twist, purl the last stitch.

Row 7: K2, P2, K3, P2, K2.

Row 8: P2, follow Steps 4-6 to make a front twist, P1, then follow Steps 1-3 to make a back twist, purl the last 2 stitches.

Instructions continued on page 8.

Step 3

Step 4

Step 5

Step 6

Photo A

Row 9: K3, P2, K1, P2, K3.

Row 10: P3, K2, P1, K2, P3.

Row 11: K3, P2, K1, P2, K3.

Let's work a popcorn in the next row like the one featured in Adult Raglan Cardigan, page 50. This popcorn will actually take two rows to complete, Row 12 to increase and Row 13 to decrease.

Row 12 (Popcorn increase row)**:**

P3, K2 then

All in the next stitch, K, K1 through the back loop ***(Fig. A)***, K, K1 through the back loop, K: 5 stitches in one stitch ***(Fig. B)***. K2, P3 to finish the row.

Row 13 (Popcorn decrease row)**:**
K3, P2, then

Knit the 5 stitches of the popcorn together through the back loop ***(Fig. C)***.

then P2, K3 to finish the row ***(Photo B)***.

Let's get a little distance so that you can work a bobble. A bobble is bigger than a popcorn, yet it is completed in one row by increasing, then turning to work across the bobble's stitches.

Row 14: P3, K2, P1, K2, P3.

Row 15: K3, P2, K1, P2, K3.

Fig. A

Fig. B

Fig. C

Photo B

Row 16 (Bobble row)**:**
P3, K2,

then

Step 1: All in the next st [K1, YO *(Fig. 7a, page 72)*, K1, YO, K1]: 5 stitches in one stitch.

Step 2: Turn; purl across the 5 bobble sts.

Step 3: Turn; knit across the 5 bobble sts.

Step 4: With the left needle, pass the last bobble st over the first 4 sts and off the needle.

Step 5: Separately pass the last bobble st over the others and off the needle until only one is left.

The bobble is complete, so K2, P3 to finish the row *(Photo C)*.

You've been cabling, twisting, popcorning and bobbling. See, we ***told*** you that they weren't so hard. Dive right in and start a project or turn the page for more information about cables and charts.

Photo C

Step 1

Step 2

Step 3

Step 4

Step 5

MORE CABLE INFORMATION

FRONT/LEFT/RIGHT/BACK?

Does it matter on which side of the work that the stitches are held?
If the stitches are held in the front, the cable is considered a ***front*** cable or a ***left*** crossing cable; if held in the back, a ***back*** cable or ***right*** crossing cable results.

CHARTS

On the six stitch cables pictured on this page, we have shaded one repeat of each chart to show how the charts relate to the actual stitches. They reflect the direction of the cables with right slanting lines for a back cable and left slanting lines for a front cable. Note that the cable symbol will cover all the boxes of the stitches that are used (4, 6, 8, etc.).

Symbols used to indicate knit stitches aren't standardized, but each pattern should have a key to define the stitch symbols. The symbols used in this leaflet may mean something else in some other publication, so be aware of the keys and their definitions. For example, many charts use a blank square as the symbol for both a knit stitch on the right side and a purl stitch on the wrong side. We have used a more visual symbol of a bold vertical line for a right side knit stitch and a lighter vertical line for a wrong side purl stitch. This way the chart will appear similar to the public side of the knit fabric.

While the Napkin Ring could be worked in its entirety from the chart, our other projects will have only the cabled areas charted.

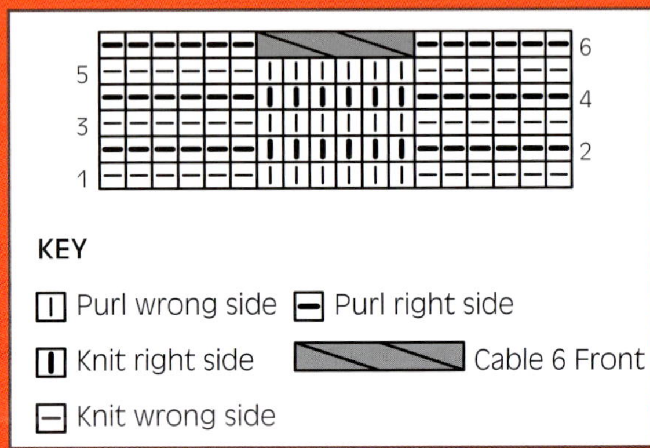

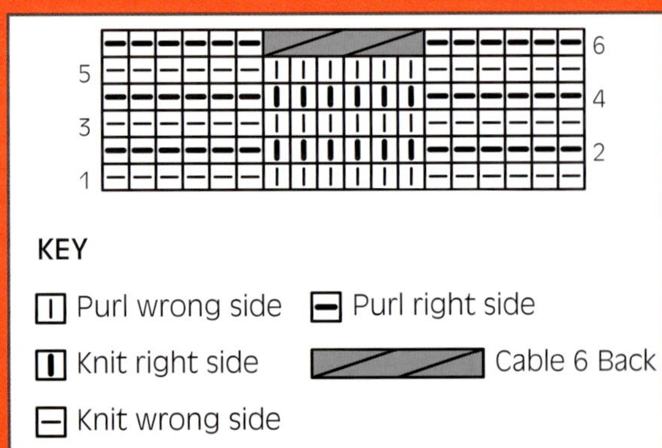

CABLE AND TWIST NAMES

Cables and twists usually have a number assigned to their definition that indicates the amount of stitches that are used to complete the pattern. These definitions are expressed in various ways; "C 2/2 Right" and "C4B" are the same cable—four stitches with the first two being held in the back. If the cable or twist is the only one used in your pattern, you may be instructed to "work cable" or "work twist."

How often should the cables twist?

The rule of thumb for standard cables is to work as many rows before twisting as you have stitches in the cable. In other words, a six stitch cable would twist on each sixth row, a four stitch on the fourth row. This allows room for the cable to relax. You may prefer a looser version of cables; in that case, add two spacer rows before the twist—the six stitch cable would twist on the eighth row and the four stitch on the sixth row and so on.

Can I just add a cable to a sweater pattern that doesn't have one?

Adding a cable to a plain sweater front involves more than just knitting it in. All this twisting affects the density and the width of your knitting. Cables pull in the width and, the more cables you have, the more width your piece will lose. Your side seams would move forward and the chest area could possibly become too tight as a result. You need to swatch the cable first to find its width vs. the amount of stitches that it uses, then compensate by adding more stitches on a row before starting the cable pattern rows. This way the front will be the proper size despite having more stitches than the plain back.

The reverse is also true. If you switch from a cable to another stitch pattern, you may have to decrease across the cable area to prevent puckering in the fabric. An example of this would be a turtleneck that has a cable that travels all the way up the neck to the bind off round. The Cable and Rib Shell on page 40 is an example of this. When binding off the stitches that form the cable, it is recommended to decrease some of them first rather than just knitting them as you would normally do before binding them off. You would K2 tog or P2 tog (whichever is applicable), then bind off the resulting stitch. Doing this will stop those stitches from flaring out along the neck edge.

Now that you've learned all the ins and outs of cables, you've also finished your first project! The next design is a pair of baby booties with a sweet little cable running through them. Choose these for your second project, or move ahead to any of the remaining patterns. The fun of adding elegance and motion to your knitting has only just begun!

BOOTIES

EASY

Finished Size: Newborn to 3 months

MATERIALS

Light Weight Yarn (LIGHT 3)
55 yards (50 meters)
Straight knitting needles, size 5 (3.75 mm) **or** size needed for gauge
Stitch holders - 3
Cable needle
Yarn needle
1/4" (7 mm) Ribbon - 1 yard (1 meter)

GAUGE: In Stockinette Stitch,
12 sts = 2" (5 cm)

STITCH GUIDE

CABLE 4 BACK *(abbreviated C4B)* (uses 4 sts)
Slip 2 sts onto cable needle and hold in **back** of work, K2 from left needle, K2 from cable needle.

KEY

Purl wrong side

Knit right side

Knit wrong side

Purl right side

Cable 4 Back

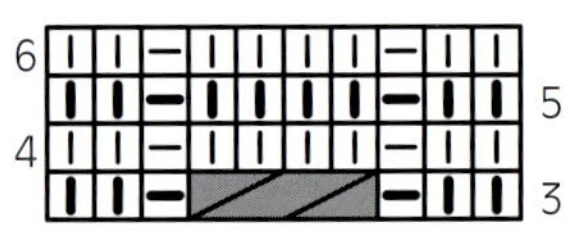

Instep panel

CUFF

Cast on 32 sts.

Rows 1-13: (K2, P2) across.

Row 14: K7, [slip 1 as if to **knit**, K1, PSSO ***(Figs. 10a & b, page 74)***], [K6, K2 tog ***(Fig. 8, page 73)***] twice, K7: 29 sts.

Row 15 (Wrong side)**:** Purl across.

Row 16 (Eyelet row)**:** K1, [YO ***(Fig. 7a, page 72)***, K2 tog] across.

Row 17: Purl across.

INSTEP

Row 1: K 10, slip sts just worked onto st holder, K2, P1, increase ***(Figs. 2a & b, page 71)***, K2, P1, K2, slip last 10 sts onto second st holder: 10 sts.

Row 2: P2, K1, P4, K1, P2.

Row 3: K2, P1, C4B, P1, K2.

Row 4: P2, K1, P4, K1, P2.

Row 5: K2, P1, K4, P1, K2.

Row 6: P2, K1, P4, K1, P2.

Rows 7-18: Repeat Rows 3-6, 3 times.

Slip sts onto third st holder; cut yarn.

SIDES

Row 1: With **right** side facing, slip 10 sts from first st holder onto empty needle, pick up 9 sts evenly spaced along right side of Instep ***(Fig. 14b, page 76)***, K2, P1, K4, P1, K2 from Instep st holder, pick up 9 sts evenly spaced along left side of Instep, slip 10 sts from last st holder onto empty needle and knit across: 48 sts.

Row 2: P 21, K1, P4, K1, P 21.

Row 3: K 20, K2 tog, K4, K2 tog, K 20: 46 sts.

Row 4: Purl across.

Row 5: Knit across.

Rows 6-10: Repeat Rows 4 and 5 twice, then repeat Row 4 once **more**.

SOLE

Row 1 (Right side)**:** Slip 1 as if to **knit**, K1, PSSO, K 18, slip 1 as if to **knit**, K1, PSSO, K2, K2 tog, K 18, K2 tog: 42 sts.

Row 2: Purl across.

Row 3: Slip 1 as if to **knit**, K1, PSSO, K 16, slip 1 as if to **knit**, K1, PSSO, K2 tog twice, K 16, K2 tog: 37 sts.

Bind off all sts **loosely** in **purl**.

FINISHING

Sew Sole and back in one continuous seam.

Weave an 18" (45.5 cm) length of ribbon through Eyelet row.

Design by Barbara Botello.

BABY BLANKET

INTERMEDIATE

Finished Size: 30"w x 42"h
(76 cm x 106.5 cm)

MATERIALS

Medium Weight Yarn
[3.5 ounces, 171 yards
(100 grams, 156 meters) per ball]:
6 balls
Straight knitting needles, size 8 (5 mm)
or size needed for gauge
Cable needle

GAUGE: In Garter Stitch, 16 sts = 4" (10 cm)

STITCH GUIDE

LEFT TWIST *(abbreviated LT)*
(uses 2 sts)
Knit into the **back** of the second st on left needle, then **knit** the first st *(Figs. 13a & b, page 75)*, letting both sts drop off the needle at the same time.

CABLE 4 FRONT *(abbreviated C4F)*
(uses 4 sts)
Slip 2 sts onto cable needle and hold in **front** of work, K2 from left needle, K2 from cable needle.

CABLE 4 BACK *(abbreviated C4B)*
(uses 4 sts)
Slip 2 sts onto cable needle and hold in **back** of work, K2 from left needle, K2 from cable needle.

CABLE 8 FRONT *(abbreviated C8F)*
(uses 8 sts)
Slip 4 sts onto cable needle and hold in **front** of work, K4 from left needle, K4 from cable needle.

CABLE 8 BACK *(abbreviated C8B)*
(uses 8 sts)
Slip 4 sts onto cable needle and hold in **back** of work, K4 from left needle, K4 from cable needle.

KEY

Purl wrong side

Knit right side

Knit wrong side

Purl right side

Left Twist

Cable 4 Front

Cable 4 Back

Cable 8 Front

Cable 8 Back

Center Panel Repeat

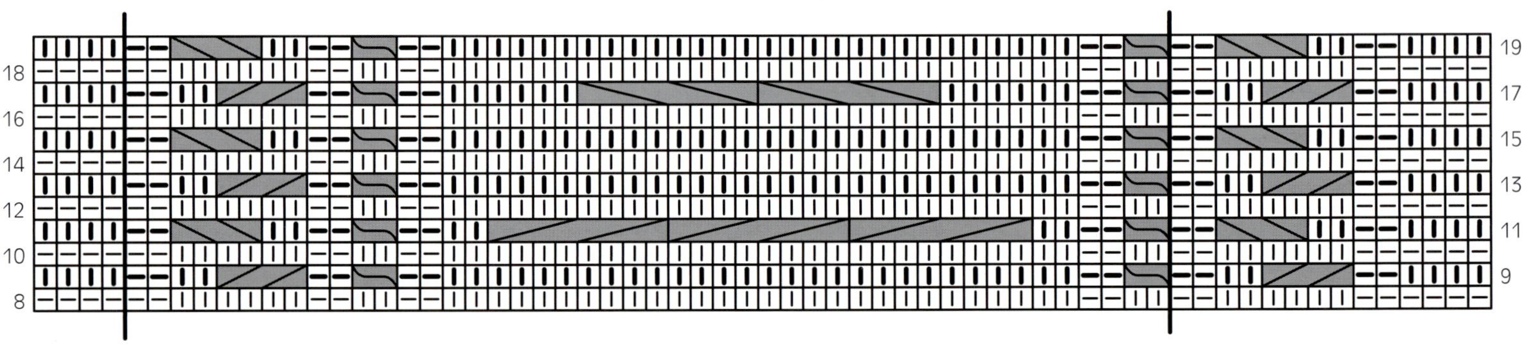

Instructions begin on page 16.

BLANKET

Cast on 121 sts.

Rows 1-5: Knit across.

Row 6: K7, M1 ***(Figs. 3a & b, page 71)***, K1, M1, K9, ★ † M1, (K2, M1) 8 times, K9, M1, K1, M1 †, K9; repeat from ★ once **more**, then repeat from † to † once, K8: 156 sts.

Row 7 (Right side)**:** K4, P2, K6, P2, ★ K2, P2, K 28, P2, K2, P2, K6, P2; repeat from ★ 2 times **more**, K4.

Row 8 AND ALL WRONG SIDE ROWS: K6, P6, ★ K2, P2, K2, P 28, K2, P2, K2, P6; repeat from ★ 2 times **more**, K6.

Row 9: K4, P2, C4B, K2, P2, ★ LT ***(Figs. 13a & b, page 75)***, P2, K 28, P2, LT, P2, C4B, K2, P2; repeat from ★ 2 times **more**, K4.

Row 11: K4, P2, K2, C4F, P2, ★ LT, P2, K2, C8B 3 times, K2, P2, LT, P2, K2, C4F, P2; repeat from ★ 2 times **more**, K4.

Row 13: K4, P2, C4B, K2, P2, ★ LT, P2, K 28, P2, LT, P2, C4B, K2, P2; repeat from ★ 2 times **more**, K4.

Row 15: K4, P2, K2, C4F, P2, ★ LT, P2, K 28, P2, LT, P2, K2, C4F, P2; repeat from ★ 2 times **more**, K4.

Row 17: K4, P2, C4B, K2, P2, ★ LT, P2, K6, C8F twice, K6, P2, LT, P2, C4B, K2, P2; repeat from ★ 2 times **more**, K4.

Row 19: K4, P2, K2, C4F, P2, ★ LT, P2, K 28, P2, LT, P2, K2, C4F, P2; repeat from ★ 2 times **more**, K4

Repeat Rows 8-19 for pattern until Blanket measures approximately 41" (104 cm) from cast on edge, ending by working Row 10 or 16.

Next Row: K7, K2 tog ***(Fig. 8, page 73)***, K1, K2 tog, ★ K7, K2 tog, (K1, K2 tog) 8 times, K8, K2 tog, K1, K2 tog; repeat from ★ 2 times **more**, K6: 121 sts.

Last 4 Rows: Knit across.

Bind off all sts in **knit**.

Design by Katie Galucki and Sarah J. Green.

BABY V-NECK CARDIGAN

Shown on page 19.

INTERMEDIATE

Size	**Finished Chest Measurement**
1	$22^{1}/_{2}$" (57 cm)
2	$23^{1}/_{4}$" (59 cm)
4	24" (61 cm)

Size Note: Instructions are written for size 1 with sizes 2 and 4 in braces { }. Instructions will be easier to read if you circle all the numbers pertaining to your size. If only one number is given, it applies to all sizes.

MATERIALS

Light Weight Yarn (LIGHT 3)
[5 ounces, 455 yards
(140 grams, 416 meters) per ball]:
1{2-2} ball(s)
Straight knitting needles, sizes 4 (3.5 mm) **and** 6 (4 mm) **or** sizes needed for gauge
Cable needle
Markers
Tapestry needle
$^{1}/_{2}$" (12 mm) Buttons - 4
Sewing needle and thread

GAUGE: With larger size needles, in Stockinette Stitch, 22 sts and 28 rows = 4" (10 cm)

STITCH GUIDE

RIGHT TWIST *(abbreviated RT)* (uses 2 sts)
Knit into the **front** of the second st on the left needle, then **knit** the first st ***(Figs. 12a & b, page 75)***, letting both sts drop off the needle at the same time.

CABLE 4 BACK *(abbreviated C4B)* (uses 4 sts)
Slip 2 sts onto cable needle and hold in **back** of work, K2 from left needle, K2 from cable needle.

CABLE 4 FRONT *(abbreviated C4F)* (uses 4 sts)
Slip 2 sts onto cable needle and hold in **front** of work, K2 from left needle, K2 from cable needle.

KEY

- Purl wrong side
- Knit right side
- Knit wrong side
- Purl right side
- Right Twist
- Cable 4 Back
- Cable 4 Front

Cable Panel Repeat

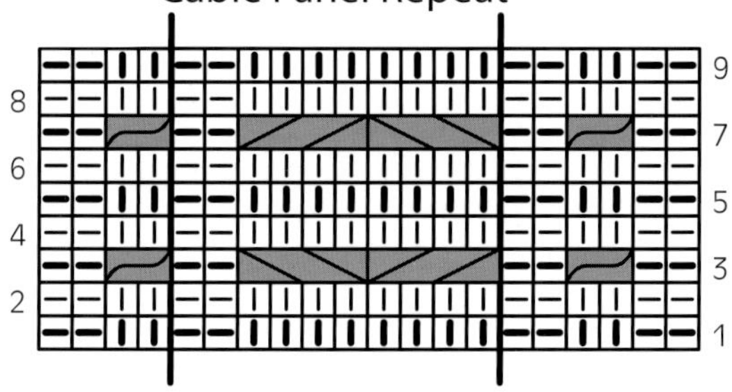

Instructions begin on page 18.

BACK

TWISTED RIBBING

With smaller size needles, cast on 63{65-67} sts.

Row 1: P1, **[**K1 tbl ***(Fig. 1, page 70)***, P1**]** across.

Row 2 (Right side)**:** K1 tbl, (P1, K1 tbl) across.

Rows 3-10: Repeat Rows 1 and 2, 4 times.

Row 11 (Increase row)**:** Increase ***(Figs. 2a & b, page 71)***, work across in established ribbing: 64{66-68} sts.

BODY

Change to larger size needles.

Rows 1 and 2: (P1, K1) across.

Rows 3 and 4: (K1, P1) across.

Repeat Rows 1-4 for pattern until Back measures $7^1/_2\{8^1/_2-9^1/_2\}$"/19{21.5-24} cm from cast on edge, ending by working a **wrong** side row.

ARMHOLE SHAPING

Maintain established pattern throughout.

Rows 1 and 2: Bind off 4 sts at the beginning of the next 2 rows, work across: 56{58-60} sts.

Work even until Armholes measure $4\{4^3/_4-5^1/_4\}$"/10{12-13.5} cm, ending by working a **wrong** side row.

NECK SHAPING

Row 1: Work across 17{17-18} sts, bind off next 22{24-24} sts, work across: 17{17-18} sts **each** side.

Both sides of Neck are worked at the same time, using separate yarn for **each** side.

Rows 2 and 3: Work across to within 2 sts of Neck edge, decrease ***(see Decreases, pages 73 and 74)***; with second yarn, decrease, work across: 15{15-16} sts **each** side.

Row 4: Work across; with second yarn, work across.

Bind off remaining sts.

LEFT FRONT

TWISTED RIBBING

With smaller size needles, cast on 34{36-36} sts.

Row 1: K1, P1, (K1 tbl, P1) across.

Row 2 (Right side)**:** K1 tbl, (P1, K1 tbl) across to last st, K1.

Rows 3-10: Repeat Rows 1 and 2, 4 times.

Row 11 (Increase row)**:** K1, P1, (K1 tbl, P1) 2{3-2} times, increase 5{5-7} times, P1, K1 tbl, P1, (increase, P1, K1 tbl, P1) 3 times, increase 3 times, P1, K1 tbl, P1, increase, P1: 46{48-50} sts.

Instructions continued on page 20.

BODY

Change to larger size needles.

When instructed to slip a stitch, always slip as if to **purl**.

Row 1 (Right side)**:** P1, (K1, P1) twice, WYB slip 1, P2, K2, P2, (K8, P2) twice, K2, P2, WYB slip 1, P1, (K1, P1) 1{2-3} times, place marker ***(see Markers, page 70)***, **[**K1 tbl, (P1, K1 tbl) twice, K1 (Band)**]**.

Row 2: K1, P1, (K1 tbl, P1) twice, (K1, P1) 2{3-4} times, K2, P2, K2, (P8, K2) twice, P2, K2, (P1, K1) 3 times.

Row 3: K1, (P1, K1) twice, WYB slip 1, P2, RT ***(Figs. 12a & b, page 75)***, P2, (C4B, C4F, P2) twice, RT, P2, WYB slip 1, K1, (P1, K1) across to marker, K1 tbl, (P1, K1 tbl) twice, K1.

Row 4: K1, (P1, K1 tbl) twice, P2, K1, (P1, K1) 0{1-2} times ***(see Zeros, page 70)***, (P2, K2) twice, (P8, K2) twice, P2, K2, P2, (K1, P1) twice.

Row 5: P1, (K1, P1) twice, WYB slip 1, P2, K2, P2, (K8, P2) twice, K2, P2, WYB slip 1, P1, (K1, P1) across to marker, K1 tbl, (P1, K1 tbl) twice, K1.

Row 6: Repeat Row 2.

Row 7: K1, (P1, K1) twice, WYB slip 1, P2, RT, P2, (C4F, C4B, P2) twice, RT, P2, WYB slip 1, K1, (P1, K1) across to marker, K1 tbl, (P1, K1 tbl) twice, K1.

Rows 8 and 9: Repeat Rows 4 and 5.

Repeat Rows 2-9 for pattern until Left Front measures same as Back to Armhole Shaping, ending by working a **wrong** side row.

NECK AND ARMHOLE SHAPING

Maintain established pattern throughout.

Row 1: Bind off 4 sts, work across to within 2 sts of marker, decrease, work across: 41{43-45} sts.

Row 2 (Decrease row)**:** Work across to marker, decrease, work across: 40{42-44} sts.

Continue to decrease one stitch at Neck edge, every row, 3{1-1} time(s) **more**; then decrease every other row, 10{14-15} times: 27{27-28} sts.

Work even until Left Front measures same as Back, ending by working a **right** side row.

Decrease Row: K1, (P1, K1 tbl) twice, P4{4-5}, K2 tog ***(Fig. 8, page 73)***, P3, P2 tog ***(Fig. 11, page 74)***, P3, K2 tog, P2 tog, K2 tog, P2: 22{22-23} sts.

Next Row: Bind off 15{15-16} sts, work across: 7 sts.

Work even until Band measures $2^{1}/_{4}\{2^{1}/_{2}-2^{1}/_{2}\}$" /5.5{6.5-6.5} cm from bound off edge.

Bind off remaining sts.

Mark Band for 4 buttons. Place first button $^{1}/_{2}$" (12 mm) above cast on edge and last button at beginning of Neck Shaping. Space remaining 2 buttons evenly.

RIGHT FRONT

TWISTED RIBBING

With smaller size needles, cast on 34{36-36} sts.

Row 1: P1, (K1 tbl, P1) across to last st, K1.

Row 2 (Right side)**:** K1, K1 tbl, (P1, K1 tbl) across.

Row 3: P1, (K1 tbl, P1) across to last st, K1.

Row 4 (Buttonhole row)**:** K1, K1 tbl, **[**P2 tog, YO ***(Fig. 7b, page 72)***, **(Buttonhole made)]**, (P1, K1 tbl) across.

Work remaining Buttonholes in same manner to match button placement on Left Front.

Rows 5-10: Repeat Rows 1 and 2, 3 times.

Row 11 (Increase row)**:** P1, increase, P1, K1 tbl, P1, increase 3 times, P1, K1 tbl, P1, (increase, P1, K1 tbl, P1) 3 times, increase 5{5-7} times, P1, (K1 tbl, P1) 2{3-2} times, K1: 46{48-50} sts.

BODY

Change to larger size needles.

When instructed to slip a stitch, always slip as if to **purl**.

Row 1 (Right side)**: [**K1, K1 tbl, (P1, K1 tbl) twice (Band)**]**, place marker, P1, (K1, P1) 1{2-3} time(s), WYB slip 1, P2, K2, P2, (K8, P2) twice, K2, P2, WYB slip 1, P1, (K1, P1) twice.

Instructions continued on page 22.

Row 2: (K1, P1) 3 times, K2, P2, K2, (P8, K2) twice, P2, K2, (P1, K1) across to marker, P1, (K1 tbl, P1) twice, K1.

Row 3: K1, K1 tbl, (P1, K1 tbl) twice, K1, (P1, K1) 1{2-3} time(s), WYB slip 1, P2, RT, P2, (C4B, C4F, P2) twice, RT, P2, WYB slip 1, K1, (P1, K1) twice.

Row 4: (P1, K1) twice, (P2, K2) twice, (P8, K2) twice, P2, K2, P2, K1, (P1, K1) 0{1-2} time(s), P2, (K1 tbl, P1) twice, K1.

Row 5: K1, K1 tbl, (P1, K1 tbl) twice, P1, (K1, P1) 1{2-3} time(s), WYB slip 1, P2, K2, P2, (K8, P2) twice, K2, P2, WYB slip 1, P1, (K1, P1) twice.

Row 6: Repeat Row 2.

Row 7: K1, K1 tbl, (P1, K1 tbl) twice, K1, (P1, K1) 1{2-3} time(s), WYB slip 1, P2, RT, P2, (C4F, C4B, P2) twice, RT, P2, WYB slip 1, K1, (P1, K1) twice.

Rows 8 and 9: Repeat Rows 4 and 5.

Repeat Rows 2-9 for pattern until Right Front measures same as Back to Armhole Shaping, ending by working a **wrong** side row.

NECK AND ARMHOLE SHAPING

Maintain established pattern throughout.

Row 1: Work to marker, decrease, work across: 45{47-49} sts.

Row 2: Bind off 4 sts, work to within 2 sts of marker, decrease, work across: 40{42-44} sts.

Row 3: Work to marker, decrease, work across: 39{41-43} sts.

Continue to decrease one stitch at Neck edge, every row, 2{0-0} times **more**; then decrease every other row, 10{14-15} times: 27{27-28} sts.

Work even until Right Front measures same as Back, ending by working a **wrong** side row.

Decrease Row: K1, K1 tbl, (P1, K1 tbl) twice, K3{3-4}, P2 tog, K3, K2 tog, K3, P2 tog, K2 tog, P2 tog, WYB slip 1, K1: 22{22-23} sts.

Next Row: Bind off 15{15-16} sts, work across: 7 sts.

Work even until Band measures $2^{1}/_{4}\{2^{1}/_{2}-2^{1}/_{2}\}$" /5.5{6.5-6.5} cm from bound off edge.

Bind off remaining sts.

Sew shoulder seams.

SLEEVE

BODY

With **right** side facing and larger size needles, pick up 51{59-65} sts evenly spaced between bound off sts ***(Fig. 14b, page 76)***, do **not** pick up bound off sts.

Rows 1 and 2: K1, (P1, K1) across.

Rows 3 and 4: P1, (K1, P1) across.

Rows 5-7: Repeat Rows 1-3.

Row 8 (Decrease row)**:** SSK ***(Figs. 9a-c, page 73)***, P1, (K1, P1) across to last 2 sts, K2 tog: 49{57-63} sts.

Maintaining established pattern, continue to decrease one stitch at **each** edge, every fourth row, 5{9-12} times; then decrease every other row, 3{2-1} times: 33{35-37} sts.

Work even until Sleeve measures $6^{1}/_{4}\{8^{1}/_{4}-9^{3}/_{4}\}$"/16{21-25} cm, ending by working a **wrong** side row.

TWISTED RIBBING

Change to smaller size needles.

Row 1: K1 tbl, (P1, K1 tbl) across.

Row 2: P1, (K1 tbl, P1) across.

Repeat Rows 1 and 2 until Ribbing measures $1^{1}/_{4}$" (3 cm), ending by working Row 2.

Bind off all sts **loosely** in pattern.

Repeat for second Sleeve.

FINISHING

Sew Bands together. Sew Band to Back Neck edge. Sew sides of Sleeve to underarm bind off.

Sew underarm and side in one continuous seam.

Sew buttons to Band opposite Buttonholes.

Design by Carole Prior.

BABY PULLOVER

INTERMEDIATE

Size	Finished Chest Measurement
1	21" (53.5 cm)
2	22" (56 cm)
4	23" (58.5 cm)

Size Note: Instructions are written for size 1 with sizes 2 and 4 in braces { }. Instructions will be easier to read if you circle all the numbers pertaining to your size. If only one number is given, it applies to all sizes.

MATERIALS

Light Weight Yarn (LIGHT 3)
[5 ounces, 459 yards
(140 grams, 420 meters) per ball]:
1{1-2} ball(s)
Straight knitting needles, sizes 4 (3.5 mm) **and** 6 (4 mm) **or** sizes needed for gauge
16" (40.5 cm) Circular knitting needle, size 4 (3.5 mm)
Stitch holders - 4
Cable needle
Markers
Tapestry needle

GAUGE: With larger size needles, in Stockinette Stitch,
22 sts and 28 rows = 4" (10 cm)

STITCH GUIDE

CABLE 4 BACK *(abbreviated C4B)* (uses 4 sts)
Slip 2 sts onto cable needle and hold in **back** of work, K2 from left needle, K2 from cable needle.

CABLE 4 FRONT *(abbreviated C4F)* (uses 4 sts)
Slip 2 sts onto cable needle and hold in **front** of work, K2 from left needle, K2 from cable needle.

TWIST 4 FRONT *(abbreviated T4F)* (uses 4 sts)
Slip 2 sts onto cable needle and hold in **front** of work, P2 from left needle, K2 from cable needle.

TWIST 4 BACK *(abbreviated T4B)* (uses 4 sts)
Slip 2 sts onto cable needle and hold in **back** of work, K2 from left needle, P2 from cable needle.

KEY

- Purl wrong side
- Knit right side
- Knit wrong side
- Purl right side
- Cable 4 Back
- Cable 4 Front
- Twist 4 Front
- Twist 4 Back

Cable Panel

Instructions begin on page 26.

BACK

RIBBING

With smaller size needles, cast on 58{62-66} sts.

Row 1: P2, (K2, P2) across.

Row 2 (Right side)**:** K2, (P2, K2) across.

Repeat Rows 1 and 2 until Ribbing measures 1½" (4 cm), ending by working Row 2.

Size 1 Only - Next Row: Work across in established ribbing increasing 2 sts evenly spaced ***(Figs. 2a & b, page 71)***: 60 sts.

Sizes 2 and 4 Only - Next Row: P2, (K2, P2) across.

BODY- All Sizes

Change to larger size needles.

Beginning with a **knit** row, work in Stockinette Stitch (knit one row, purl one row) for 42{50-54} rows.

RAGLAN SHAPING

Rows 1 and 2: Bind off 2 sts at the beginning of the next 2 rows, work across: 56{58-62} sts.

Row 3: K1, slip 1 as if to **purl**, knit across to last 2 sts, slip 1 as if to **purl**, K1.

Row 4: Purl across.

Row 5 (Decrease row)**:** K1, **[**slip 1 as if to **knit**, K1, PSSO ***(Figs. 10a & b, page 74)*****]**, knit across to last 3 sts, K2 tog ***(Fig. 8, page 73)***, K1: 54{56-60} sts.

Row 6: Purl across.

Repeat Rows 3-6, 3{4-4} times: 48{48-52} sts.

Repeat Rows 5 and 6, 10{10-11} times: 28{28-30} sts.

Slip remaining sts onto st holder.

FRONT

RIBBING

With smaller size needles, cast on 58{62-66} sts.

Row 1: P2, (K2, P2) across.

Row 2 (Right side)**:** K2, (P2, K2) across.

Repeat Rows 1 and 2 until Ribbing measures 1½" (4 cm), ending by working Row 2.

Sizes 1 and 4 Only - Increase Row: (P2, K2) 2{4} times, (increase, P1, K2) 2{1} time(s), increase twice, K2, P2, (K2, increase twice) 3 times, K2, P2, K2, increase twice, (K2, P1, increase) 2{1} time(s), (K2, P2) 2{4} times: 72{78} sts.

Size 2 Only - Increase Row: P2, K2, (increase, P1, K2) 3 times, increase twice, K2, P2, K2, increase, P1, K2, (P2, K2) twice, P1, increase, K2, P2, K2, increase twice, (K2, P1, increase) 3 times, K2, P2: 74 sts.

BODY - All Sizes

Change to larger size needles.

Row 1 (Right side)**:** K 16{17-19}, place marker ***(see Markers, page 70)***, P2, K4, P2, K2, P8, C4B, P8, K2, P2, K4, P2, place marker, knit across.

Row 2: Purl across to marker, K2, P4, K2, P2, K8, P4, K8, P2, K2, P4, K2, purl across.

Row 3: Knit across to marker, P2, C4F, P2, (T4F, P4, T4B) twice, P2, C4B, P2, knit across.

Row 4: Purl across to marker, K2, P4, K4, (P2, K4) 4 times, P4, K2, purl across.

Row 5: Knit across to marker, P2, K4, P4, (T4F, T4B, P4) twice, K4, P2, knit across.

Row 6: Purl across to marker, K2, P4, K6, P4, K8, P4, K6, P4, K2, purl across.

Row 7: Knit across to marker, P2, K4, P6, C4B, P8, C4B, P6, K4, P2, knit across.

Row 8: Purl across to marker, K2, P4, K6, P4, K8, P4, K6, P4, K2, purl across.

Row 9: Knit across to marker, P2, C4F, P4, (T4B, T4F, P4) twice, C4B, P2, knit across.

Row 10: Purl across to marker, K2, P4, K4, (P2, K4) 4 times, P4, K2, purl across.

Row 11: Knit across to marker, P2, K4, P2, (T4B, P4, T4F) twice, P2, K4, P2, knit across.

Row 12: Purl across to marker, K2, P4, K2, P2, K8, P4, K8, P2, K2, P4, K2, purl across.

Row 13: Knit across to marker, P2, K4, P2, K2, P8, C4B, P8, K2, P2, K4, P2, knit across.

Rows 14 thru 38{50-50}: Repeat Rows 2-13, 2{3-3} times; then repeat Row 2 once **more**.

Sizes 1 and 4 Only
Repeat Rows 3-6.

RAGLAN SHAPING - All Sizes

Maintain established pattern throughout.

Rows 1 and 2: Bind off 2 sts at the beginning of the next 2 rows, work across: 68{70-74} sts.

Row 3: K1, slip 1 as if to **purl**, work across to last 2 sts, slip 1 as if to **purl**, K1.

Row 4: Work across.

Row 5 (Decrease row)**:** K1, slip 1 as if to **knit**, K1, PSSO, work across to last 3 sts, K2 tog, K1: 66{68-72} sts.

Row 6: Work across.

Repeat Rows 3-6, 3{4-4} times: 60{60-64} sts.

Repeat Rows 5 and 6, 3{3-4} times; then repeat Row 5 once **more**: 52{52-54} sts.

Sizes 1 and 2 Only - Decrease Row: P6, K2, P4, K6, P2 tog twice ***(Fig. 11, page 74)***, K2 tog, K4, K2 tog, P2 tog twice, K6, P4, K2, P6: 46 sts.

Size 4 Only - Decrease Row: P7, K2, P4, K2, P2, K2 tog twice, K4, P2 tog twice ***(Fig. 11, page 74)***, K4, K2 tog twice, P2, K2, P4, K2, P7: 48 sts.

NECK SHAPING - All Sizes

Both sides of Neck are worked at the same time, using separate yarn for **each** side.

Row 1: K1, slip 1 as if to **knit**, K1, PSSO, K3{3-4}, P2, K3, slip next 24 sts onto st holder; with second yarn, K3, P2, K3{3-4}, K2 tog, K1: 10{10-11} sts **each** side.

Instructions continued on page 28.

Row 2: P5{5-6}, K2, P3; with second yarn, P3, K2, P5{5-6}.

Row 3: K1, slip 1 as if to **knit**, K1, PSSO, K2{2-3}, P2, K1, K2 tog; with second yarn, slip 1 as if to **knit**, K1, PSSO, K1, P2, K2{2-3}, K2 tog, K1: 8{8-9} sts **each** side.

Row 4: P4{4-5}, K2, P2; with second yarn, P2, K2, P4{4-5}.

Row 5: K1, slip 1 as if to **knit**, K1, PSSO, K1{1-2}, P2, K2 tog; with second yarn, slip 1 as if to **knit**, K1, PSSO, P2, K1{1-2}, K2 tog, K1: 6{6-7} sts **each** side.

Row 6: P3{3-4}, K2, P1; with second yarn, P1, K2, P3{3-4}.

Row 7: K1, slip 1 as if to **knit**, K1, PSSO, K 0{0-1} ***(see Zeros, page 70)***, P1, P2 tog; with second yarn, P2 tog, P1, K 0{0-1}, K2 tog, K1: 4{4-5} sts **each** side.

Row 8: P2{2-3}, K2; with second yarn, K2, P2{2-3}.

Row 9: K1, slip 1 as if to **knit**, K1, PSSO, P1{1-0}, P2 tog 0{0-1} time(s); with second yarn, P2 tog 0{0-1} time(s), P1{1-0}, K2 tog, K1: 3 sts **each** side.

Row 10: P1{1-2}, K2{2-1}; with second yarn, K2{2-1}, P1{1-2}.

Row 11: K1, slip 1 as if to **knit**, K1, PSSO; with second yarn, K2 tog, K1: 2 sts **each** side.

Row 12: P2 tog, cut yarn and pull through last st; with second yarn, P2 tog, cut yarn and pull through last st.

SLEEVE (Make 2)

RIBBING

With smaller size needles, cast on 34{34-38} sts.

Row 1: P2, (K2, P2) across.

Row 2 (Right side)**:** K2, (P2, K2) across.

Repeat Rows 1 and 2 until Ribbing measures 1½" (4 cm), ending by working Row 2.

Increase Row: Work across in established ribbing increasing 4 sts evenly spaced: 38{38-42} sts.

BODY

Change to larger size needles.

Row 1 (Right side)**:** K 17{17-19}, C4B, knit across.

Row 2: Purl across.

Row 3: K 15{15-17}, T4B, T4F, knit across.

Row 4: P 17{17-19}, K4, purl across.

Row 5: K 13{13-15}, T4B, P4, T4F, knit across.

Row 6: P 15{15-17}, K8, purl across.

Row 7 (Increase row)**:** Increase, K 14{14-16}, P8, knit across to last st, increase: 40{40-44} sts.

Row 8: P 16{16-18}, K8, purl across.

Row 9: K 14{14-16}, C4F, P4, C4B, knit across.

Row 10: Purl across.

Row 11: K 16{16-18}, C4F, C4B, knit across.

Row 12: Purl across.

Working in Stockinette Stitch, continue to increase one stitch at **each** edge, every sixth row, 1{3-0} time(s) **more**; then increase every eighth row, 2{2-5} times: 46{50-54} sts.

Work even until Sleeve measures 7{9-10$^{1}/_{2}$}"/ 18{23-26.5} cm from cast on edge, ending by working a **purl** row.

RAGLAN SHAPING

Rows 1 and 2: Bind off 2 sts at the beginning of the next 2 rows, work across: 42{46-50} sts.

Row 3: K1, slip 1 as if to **purl**, knit across to last 2 sts, slip 1 as if to **purl**, K1.

Row 4: Purl across.

Row 5 (Decrease row)**:** K1, slip 1 as if to **knit**, K1, PSSO, knit across to last 3 sts, K2 tog, K1: 40{44-48} sts.

Row 6: Purl across.

Repeat Rows 3-6, 1{1-0} time(s): 38{42-48} sts.

Repeat Rows 5 and 6, 14{16-19} times: 10 sts.

Slip remaining sts onto st holder.

FINISHING

Weave raglan seams ***(Fig. 15, page 76)***.

Weave underarm and side in one continuous seam.

NECK RIBBING

With **right** side facing, slip 28{28-30} sts from Back st holder onto circular needle and knit across, slip 10 sts from Sleeve st holder onto opposite end and knit across, pick up 8{8-9} sts evenly spaced along left Neck edge ***(Fig. 14b, page 76)***, slip 24 sts from Front st holder onto opposite end, K1, P2, (K2, P2) 5 times, K1, pick up 8{8-9} sts evenly spaced along right Neck edge, slip 10 sts from Sleeve st holder onto opposite end and knit across; place marker to mark beginning of rnd: 88{88-92} sts.

Work in K2, P2 ribbing around for $^{3}/_{4}$" (19 mm).

Bind off all sts **loosely** in ribbing.

Design by Carole Prior.

SCARF

EASY

Finished Size: 4"w x 54"l (10 cm x 137 cm)

MATERIALS

Fine Weight Yarn (2 FINE)
[1.75 ounces, 235 yards
(50 grams, 215 meters) per ball]: 1 ball

Straight knitting needles, size 6 (4 mm) **or** size needed for gauge

Cable needle

GAUGE: In pattern,
28 sts and 32 rows = 4" (10 cm)

KEY

- Purl wrong side
- Knit right side
- Knit wrong side
- Purl right side
- Twist 2 Front
- Twist 2 Back
- Cable 4 Back

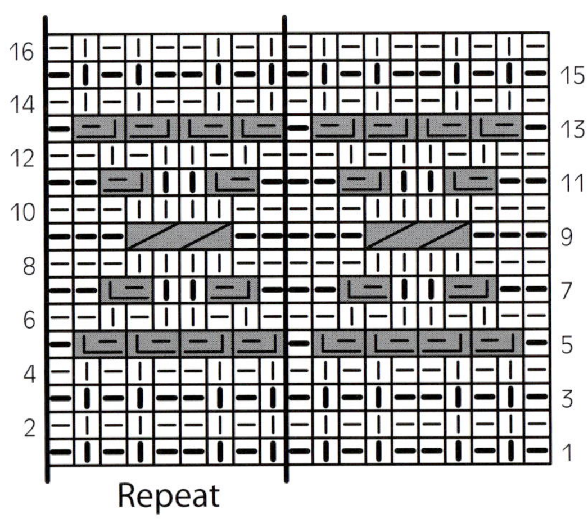

STITCH GUIDE

TWIST 2 FRONT *(abbreviated T2F)* (uses 2 sts)
Slip next st onto cable needle and hold in **front** of work, P1 from left needle, K1 from cable needle.

TWIST 2 BACK *(abbreviated T2B)* (uses 2 sts)
Slip next st onto cable needle and hold in **back** of work, K1 from left needle, P1 from cable needle.

CABLE 4 BACK *(abbreviated C4B)* (uses 4 sts)
Slip 2 sts onto cable needle and hold in **back** of work, K2 from left needle, K2 from cable needle.

SCARF

Cast on 28 sts.

Row 1 (Right side)**:** (P1, K1) twice, P2, ★ K1, (P1, K1) 3 times, P2; repeat from ★ once **more**, (K1, P1) twice.

Row 2: (K1, P1) twice, K2, ★ P1, (K1, P1) 3 times, K2; repeat from ★ once **more**, (P1, K1) twice.

Rows 3 and 4: Repeat Rows 1 and 2.

Row 5: P1, ★ T2F twice, T2B twice, P1; repeat from ★ across.

Row 6: K2, P1, K1, P2, K1, P1, ★ K3, P1, K1, P2, K1, P1; repeat from ★ once **more**, K2.

Row 7: P2, T2F, K2, T2B, ★ P3, T2F, K2, T2B; repeat from ★ once **more**, P2.

Row 8: K3, P4, (K5, P4) across to last 3 sts, K3.

Row 9: P3, C4B, (P5, C4B) twice, P3.

Row 10: Repeat Row 8.

Row 11: P2, T2B, K2, T2F, ★ P3, T2B, K2, T2F; repeat from ★ once **more**, P2.

Row 12: Repeat Row 6.

Row 13: P1, ★ T2B twice, T2F twice, P1; repeat from ★ across.

Row 14: Repeat Row 2.

Rows 15 and 16: Repeat Rows 1 and 2.

Repeat Rows 1-16 for pattern until Scarf measures 54" (137 cm) from cast on edge, ending by working Row 16.

Bind off all sts in pattern.

CAP

INTERMEDIATE

Size: Medium {Large}
Finished Size: 18{20}"/45.5{51} cm head circumference

Size Note: Instructions are written for size Medium with size Large in braces { }. Instructions will be easier to read if you circle all the numbers pertaining to your size. If only one number is given, it applies to both sizes.

MATERIALS

Medium Weight Yarn

Solid Version
[3.5 ounces, 200 yards (100 grams, 182 meters) per ball]:
Grey - 1 ball

Two Color Version
[3.5 ounces, 210 yards (100 grams, 192 meters) per ball]:
Lt Purple - 1 ball
Purple - 1 ball

Straight knitting needles, size 8 (5 mm) **or** size needed for gauge
Double pointed knitting needles, size 8 (5 mm)
Cable needle
Yarn needle

Band

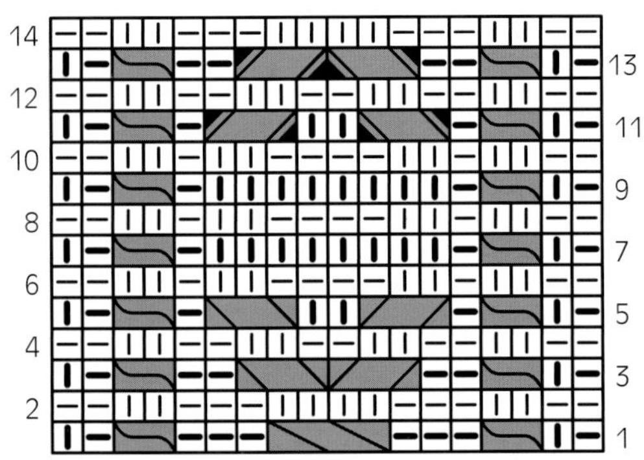

KEY

- Purl wrong side
- Knit right side
- Knit wrong side
- Purl right side
- Left Twist
- Twist 3 Front
- Twist 3 Back
- Cable 3 Back
- Cable 3 Front
- Cable 4 Front

STITCH GUIDE

TWIST 3 FRONT ***(abbreviated T3F)*** (uses 3 sts)
Slip 2 sts onto cable needle and hold in **front** of work, P1 from left needle, K2 from cable needle.

TWIST 3 BACK ***(abbreviated T3B)*** (uses 3 sts)
Slip next st onto cable needle and hold in **back** of work, K2 from left needle, P1 from cable needle.

LEFT TWIST ***(abbreviated LT)*** (uses 2 sts)
Knit into the **back** of the second st on left needle, then knit the first st ***(Figs. 13a & b, page 75)***, letting both sts drop off the needle at the same time.

CABLE 3 FRONT ***(abbreviated C3F)*** (uses 3 sts)
Slip 2 sts onto cable needle and hold in **front** of work, K1 from left needle, K2 from cable needle.

CABLE 3 BACK ***(abbreviated C3B)*** (uses 3 sts)
Slip next st onto cable needle and hold in **back** of work, K2 from left needle, K1 from cable needle.

CABLE 4 FRONT ***(abbreviated C4F)*** (uses 4 sts)
Slip 2 sts onto cable needle and hold in **front** of work, K2 from left needle, K2 from cable needle.

GAUGE: In K2, P2 ribbing (slightly stretched),
24 sts = 4" (10 cm)

BAND

With Lt Purple or Grey, cast on 18 sts.

Row 1 (Right side)**:** K1, P1, LT, P3, C4F, P3, LT, P1, K1.

Row 2: K2, P2, K3, P4, K3, P2, K2.

Row 3: K1, P1, LT, P2, C3B, C3F, P2, LT, P1, K1.

Row 4: K2, (P2, K2) across.

Row 5: K1, P1, LT, P1, C3B, K2, C3F, P1, LT, P1, K1.

Row 6: K2, P2, K1, P2, K4, P2, K1, P2, K2.

Row 7: K1, P1, LT, P1, K8, P1, LT, P1, K1.

Instructions continued on page 34.

Rows 8-10: Repeat Rows 6 and 7 once, then repeat Row 6 once **more**.

Row 11: K1, P1, LT, P1, T3F, K2, T3B, P1, LT, P1, K1.

Row 12: K2, (P2, K2) across.

Row 13: K1, P1, LT, P2, T3F, T3B, P2, LT, P1, K1.

Row 14: K2, P2, K3, P4, K3, P2, K2.

Rows 15 thru 126{140}: Repeat Rows 1-14, 8{9} times.

Bind off all sts in pattern.

Sew cast on edge to last row to form a ring.

CROWN

With **right** side facing, using double pointed needles, and Grey for the Solid Version or Purple for the Two Color Version, pick up 120{140} sts in the second st from end of rows along one edge of Band ***(Fig. A)***; place marker to mark beginning of rnd ***(see Markers, page 70)***.

Fig. A

Work around in K2, P2 ribbing until Cap measures 4{4 1/2}"/10{12} cm from bottom edge of Band.

SHAPING

Rnd 1: **[**K2, P2 tog ***(Fig. 11, page 74)*****]** around: 90{105} sts.

Rnds 2-7: (K2, P1) around.

Rnd 8: **[**K2 tog ***(Fig. 8, page 73)***, P1**]** around: 60{70} sts.

Rnds 9 and 10: (K1, P1) around.

Size Medium Only

Rnd 11: (K1, K2 tog) around: 40 sts.

Rnds 12-14: K2 tog around: 5 sts.

Cut yarn leaving a long end; thread yarn needle with end and weave through remaining sts; gather tightly and secure end.

Size Large Only

Rnd 11: (K3, K2 tog) around: 56 sts.

Rnd 12: (K2, K2 tog): 42 sts.

Rnd 13: K2 tog around: 21 sts.

Rnd 14: (K1, K2 tog) around: 14 sts.

Rnd 15: K2 tog around: 7 sts.

Cut yarn leaving a long end; thread yarn needle with end and weave through remaining sts; gather tightly and secure end.

Design by Sarah J. Green.

PURSE

Shown on page 37.

INTERMEDIATE

Finished Size: 14"w x 11"h
(35.5 cm x 28 cm)

MATERIALS

Bulky Weight Yarn BULKY 5
[3.5 ounces, 164 yards
(100 grams, 150 meters) per ball]: 3 balls
Straight knitting needles, size 10 (6 mm)
or size needed for gauge
Double pointed needles, size 10 (6 mm)
Cable needle
Yarn needle
$1^{3}/_{4}$" (4.5 cm) Rings - 2
$^{3}/_{4}$" (19 mm) Buttons - 4
$^{1}/_{2}$ yard ($^{1}/_{2}$ meter) Felt for lining
Sewing needle and thread

GAUGE: In Stockinette Stitch,
14 sts and 20 rows = 4" (10 cm)

Instructions begin on page 36.

STITCH GUIDE

CABLE 4 FRONT *(abbreviated C4F)* (uses 4 sts)
Slip 2 sts onto cable needle and hold in **front** of work, K2 from left needle, K2 from cable needle.

CABLE 4 BACK *(abbreviated C4B)* (uses 4 sts)
Slip 2 sts onto cable needle and hold in **back** of work, K2 from left needle, K2 from cable needle.

TWIST 4 FRONT *(abbreviated T4F)* (uses 4 sts)
Slip 2 sts onto cable needle and hold in **front** of work, K2 from left needle, P2 from cable needle.

TWIST 4 BACK *(abbreviated T4B)* (uses 4 sts)
Slip 2 sts onto cable needle and hold in **back** of work, P2 from left needle, K2 from cable needle.

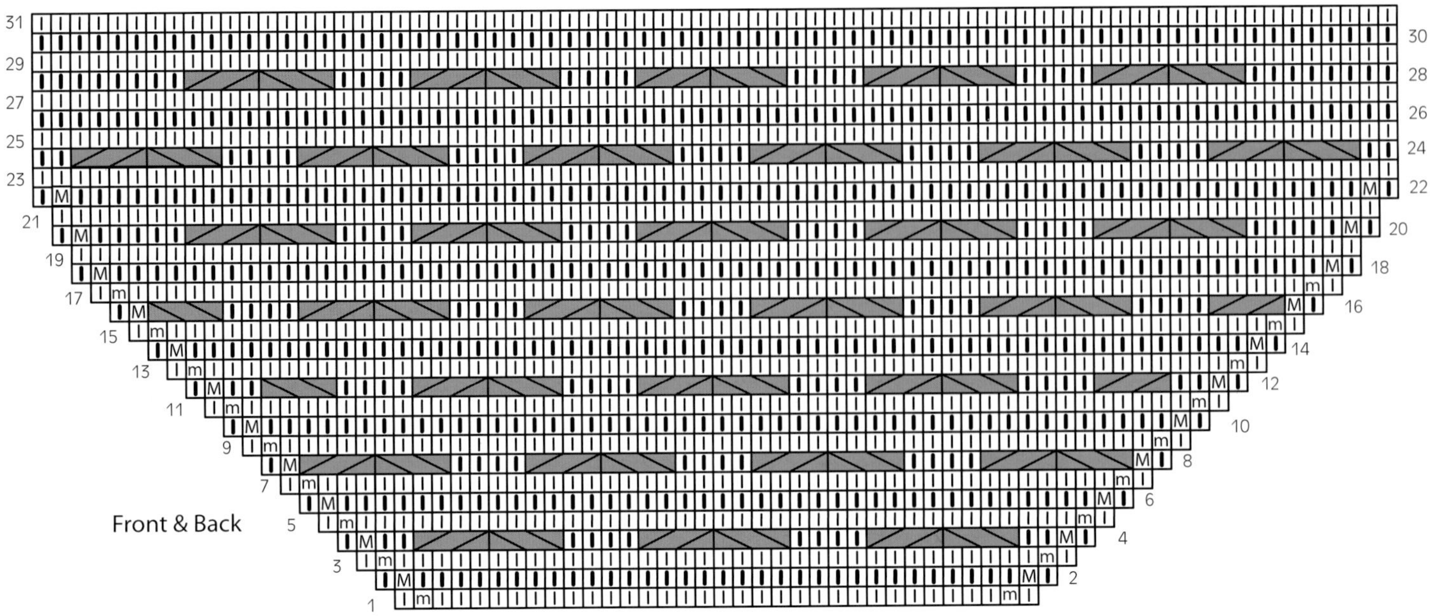

KEY

Purl wrong side

Knit right side

Make 1 knit

Make 1 purl

Cable 4 Front

Cable 4 Back

BACK

Cast on 23 sts.

Row 1: P1, [M1P ***(Figs. 5a & b, page 72)***, P2] across: 34 sts.

Row 2 (Right side)**:** K1, M1 ***(Figs. 3a & b, page 71)***, knit across to last st, M1, K1: 36 sts.

Row 3 (Increase row)**:** P1, M1P, purl across to last st, M1P, P1: 38 sts.

Row 4: K1, M1, K2, C4F, C4B, (K4, C4F, C4B) twice, K2, M1, K1: 40 sts.

Row 5: Repeat Row 3: 42 sts.

Row 6: K1, M1, knit across to last st, M1, K1: 44 sts.

Row 7: Repeat Row 3: 46 sts.

Row 8: K1, M1, C4F, C4B, (K4, C4F, C4B) 3 times, M1, K1: 48 sts.

Rows 9-11: Repeat Rows 5-7: 54 sts.

Row 12: K1, M1, K2, C4B, K4, (C4F, C4B, K4) 3 times, C4F, K2, M1, K1: 56 sts.

Rows 13-15: Repeat Rows 5-7: 62 sts.

Row 16: K1, M1, C4B, K4, (C4F, C4B, K4) 4 times, C4F, M1, K1: 64 sts.

Rows 17 and 18: Repeat Rows 5 and 6: 68 sts.

Row 19: Purl across.

Row 20: K1, M1, K5, C4F, C4B, (K4, C4F, C4B) 4 times, K5, M1, K1: 70 sts.

Row 21: Purl across.

Row 22: K1, M1, knit across to last st, M1, K1: 72 sts.

Row 23: Purl across.

Instructions continued on page 38.

Row 24: K2, C4F, C4B, (K4, C4F, C4B) 5 times, K2.

Row 25: Purl across.

Row 26: Knit across.

Row 27: Purl across.

Row 28: K8, C4F, C4B, (K4, C4F, C4B) 4 times, K8.

Rows 29-31: Repeat Rows 25-27.

Rows 32-48: Repeat Rows 24-31 twice, then repeat Row 24 once **more**.

Using Back as a pattern, cut 2 pieces from felt, $^{1}/_{4}$" (7 mm) smaller than Back.

TOP BAND

Row 1: K2, K2 tog 4 times *(Fig. 8, page 73)*, (K4, K2 tog 4 times) 5 times, K2: 48 sts.

Rows 2-4: Knit across.

Row 5: K2, purl across to last 2 sts, K2.

Row 6: Knit across.

Rows 7-10: Repeat Rows 5 and 6 twice.

Rows 11 and 12: Knit across.

Rows 13-18: Repeat Rows 5 and 6, 3 times.

Rows 19-21: Knit across.

Bind off all sts in **knit**.

Sew bound off edge to Row 1 on **wrong** side.

FRONT

Work same as Back, page 32, through Row 7 of Top Band: 48 sts.

Row 8 (Buttonhole row)**:** K5, K2 tog, YO *(Fig. 7a, page 72)*, (K 10, K2 tog, YO) 3 times, K5.

Row 9: Purl across.

Rows 10-12: Knit across.

Row 13: Purl across.

Rows 14-18: Repeat Rows 6-10.

Rows 19-21: Knit across.

Bind off all sts in **knit**.

Sew bound off edge to Row 1 on **wrong** side.

GUSSET

Cast on 14 sts.

Row 1 (Right side)**:** P3, K2, P4, K2, P3.

Row 2: K3, P2, K4, P2, K3.

Rows 3-8: Repeat Rows 1 and 2, 3 times.

Row 9: P3, T4F, T4B, P3.

Row 10: K3, P2, K4, P2, K3.

Rows 11-148: Repeat Rows 1-10, 13 times; then repeat Rows 1-8 once **more**.

Bind off all sts in pattern.

Using Gusset as a pattern, cut a piece of felt $^{1}/_{4}$" (7 mm) smaller than Gusset.

GUSSET

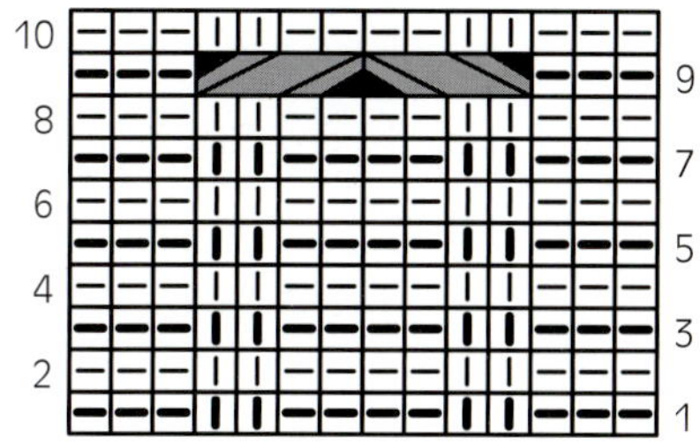

KEY

- Purl wrong side
- Knit right side
- Knit wrong side
- Purl right side
- Twist 4 Front
- Twist 4 Back

LOOP (Make 2)
Using double pointed needles, cast on 3 sts.

Row 1: K3, slide sts to opposite end of needle.

Repeat Row 1 until Loop measures 3" (7.5 cm).

Bind off all sts leaving a long end for sewing.

HANDLE STRAND (Make 3)
Using double pointed needles, cast on 3 sts. Work same as Loop until Strand measures 72" (183 cm).

Bind off all sts leaving a long end for sewing.

ASSEMBLY

Weave Gusset to Front and Back ***(Fig. 15, page 76)***, leaving a long end at each edge. Thread yarn needle with long end and gather sts tightly on short edge of Gusset; secure end. Repeat for opposite end of Gusset.

Sew lining pieces to wrong sides of Gusset, Back and Front.

Slip one ring onto each Loop, then sew ends together. Sew one Loop at each end of Gusset, then sew edges of Top Bands to Loop ***(Figs. A & B)***.

Braid Strands. Pull each end of braid through a ring and secure. Wrap a doubled strand of yarn 25 times around doubled end of braid and secure ends.

Sew through both layers on Front around buttonholes to reinforce the area.

Sew buttons to Back opposite buttonholes.

Design by Sarah J. Green.

Fig. A

Fig. B

CABLE AND RIB SHELL

INTERMEDIATE

Size	**Finished Chest Measurement**
Small	35" (89 cm)
Medium	37" (94 cm)
Large	39" (99 cm)
X-Large	$40^1/_2$" (103 cm)
2X-Large	42" (106.5 cm)

Size Note: Instructions are written with sizes Small and Medium in the first set of braces { } and sizes Large, X-Large, and 2X-Large in the second set of braces. Instructions will be easier to read if you circle all the numbers pertaining to your size. If only one number is given, it applies to all sizes.

MATERIALS

Medium Weight Yarn (MEDIUM 4)
[1.75 ounces, 61 yards (50 grams, 55 meters) per ball]:
{11-12}{13-14-15} balls

Straight knitting needles, size 6 (4 mm) **or** size needed for gauge

16" (40.5 cm) Circular knitting needle, size 6 (4 mm)

Stitch holders - 3

Cable needle

Markers

Yarn needle

GAUGE: In K2, P2 ribbing (slightly stretched), 19 sts and 32 rows = 4" (10 cm)

STITCH GUIDE

CABLE 6 BACK *(abbreviated C6B)* (uses 6 sts)
Slip 3 sts onto cable and hold in **back** of work, K3 tbl ***(Fig. 1, page 70)***, K3 tbl from cable needle.

CABLE 6 FRONT *(abbreviated C6F)* (uses 6 sts)
Slip 3 sts onto cable and hold in **front** of work, K3 tbl ***(Fig. 1, page 66)***, K3 tbl from cable needle.

KEY

| Purl wrong side

B Knit tbl right side

Cable 6 Front

Cable 6 Back

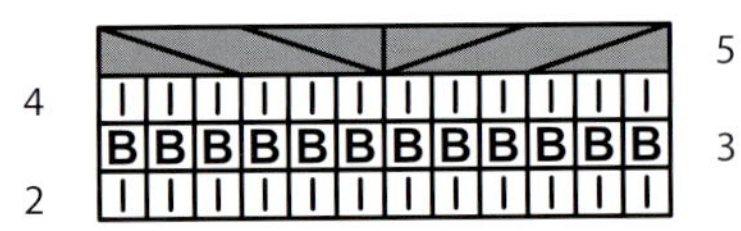

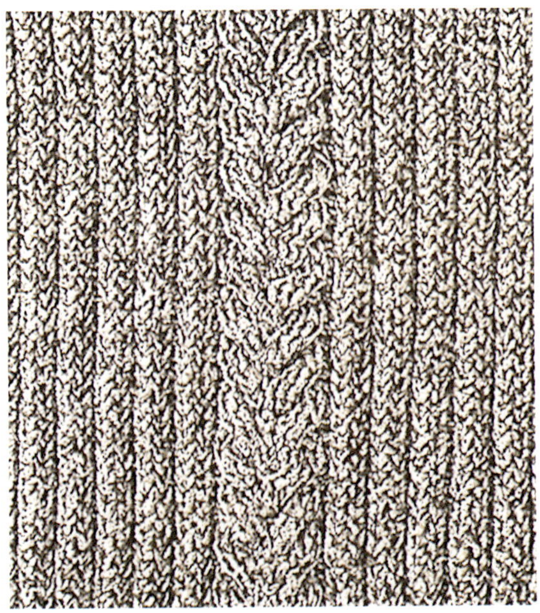

Instructions begin on page 42.

BACK

Cast on {86-90}{94-98-102} sts.

Row 1 (Right side)**:** K2, (P2, K2) across.

Row 2: P2, (K2, P2) across.

Repeat Rows 1 and 2 for pattern until Back measures {12-$12^{1}/_{2}$}{$12^{1}/_{2}$-13-13}"/ {30.5-32{32-33-33} cm from cast on edge, ending by working Row 2.

ARMHOLE SHAPING

Maintain established pattern throughout.

Rows 1 and 2: Bind off 4 sts at the beginning of the next 2 rows, work across: {78-82}{86-90-94} sts.

Row 3 (Decrease row)**:** K1, SSK ***(Figs. 9a-c, page 73)***, work across to last 3 sts, K2 tog ***(Fig. 8, page 73)***, K1: {76-80}{84-88-92} sts.

Row 4: P2, K1, P2, (K2, P2) across to last 3 sts, K1, P2.

Row 5 (Decrease row)**:** K1, SSK, work across to last 3 sts, K2 tog, K1: {74-78}{82-86-90} sts.

Row 6: P4, K2, (P2, K2) across to last 4 sts, P4.

Row 7 (Decrease row)**:** K1, SSK, work across to last 3 sts, K2 tog, K1: {72-76}{80-84-88} sts.

Row 8: P3, K2, (P2, K2) across to last 3 sts, P3.

Row 9 (Decrease row)**:** K1, SSK, work across to last 3 sts, K2 tog, K1: {70-74}{78-82-86} sts.

Row 10: P2, (K2, P2) across.

Repeat Rows 3-10 twice: {54-58}{62-66-70} sts.

Work even until Armholes measure {$7^{1}/_{2}$-$7^{1}/_{2}$}{8-8-$8^{1}/_{2}$}"/{19-19}{20.5-20.5-21.5} cm, ending by working a **wrong** side row.

Slip remaining sts onto st holder.

FRONT

Cast on {84-92}{100-100-108} sts.

Row 1 (Right side)**:** (K2, P2) {9-10}{11-11-12} times, place marker ***(see Markers, page 70)***, K 12 tbl ***(Fig. 1, page 70)***, place marker, (P2, K2) across.

Row 2: (P2, K2) across to marker, P 12, (K2, P2) across.

Row 3: (K2, P2) across to marker, K 12 tbl, (P2, K2) across.

Row 4: (P2, K2) across to marker, P 12, (K2, P2) across.

Row 5: (K2, P2) across to marker, C6B, C6F, (P2, K2) across.

Repeat Rows 2-5 for pattern until Front measures same as Back to Armhole Shaping.

ARMHOLE SHAPING

Maintaining center 12 sts in established pattern, work same as Back until Armholes measure 5" (12.5 cm), ending by working Row 4: {52-60}{68-68-76} sts.

NECK SHAPING

Row 1: K2, (P2, K2) across to within 6 sts of marker, P1, K2 tog, K1, P2, remove marker, C6B, C6F, remove marker, P2, K1, SSK, P1, K2, (P2, K2) across: {50-58}{66-66-74} sts.

Row 2: P2, (K2, P2) 3{4-5-6-7} times, K1, P2, K2, P 12, K2, slip 16 sts just worked onto st holder, P2, K1, P2, (K2, P2) across: {17-21}{25-25-29} sts **each** side.

Both sides of Neck are worked at the same time, using separate yarn for each side. Maintain established pattern throughout.

Row 3 (Decrease row)**:** (K2, P2) {3-4}{5-6-7} times, K1, K2 tog, K1, P1; with second yarn, P1, K1, SSK, K1, (P2, K2) across: {16-20}{24-24-28} sts **each** side.

Row 4: Work across; with second yarn, work across.

Row 5 (Decrease row)**:** Work across to last 4 sts, K2 tog, K1, P1; with second yarn, P1, K1, SSK, (P2, K2) across: {15-19}{23-23-27} sts **each** side..

Repeat Rows 4 and 5, {0-4}{8-4-8} times ***(see Zeros, page 70)***: {15-15}{15-19-19} sts **each** side.

Work even until Front measures same as Back, ending by working a **wrong** side row.

Slip remaining sts onto st holders.

FINISHING

Join Front to Back using 3-Needle Bind-Off ***(Fig. 16, page 76)***, leaving center {24-28}{32-28-32} sts on Back st holder.

MOCK TURTLENECK

With **right** side facing, using circular needle, and beginning at left shoulder seam, pick up {15-15}{19-23-23} sts evenly spaced along left Front Neck edge ***(Fig. 14b, page 76)***, place marker, slip 16 sts from Front st holder onto opposite end, P2, K 12 tbl, P2, pick up {15-15}{19-23-23} sts evenly spaced along right Front Neck edge, slip {24-28}{32-28-32} sts from Back st holder onto opposite end, P1, K2, (P2, K2) across to last st, P1; place marker: {70-74}{86-90-94} sts.

Rnd 1: P1, K2, (P2, K2) around to first marker, P2, K 12, (P2, K2) around to last st, P1.

Rnd 2: P1, K2, (P2, K2) around to first marker, P2, C6B, C6F, (P2, K2) around to last st, P1.

Rnd 3: P1, K2, (P2, K2) around to first marker, P2, K 12, (P2, K2) around to last st, P1.

Rnd 4: P1, K2, (P2, K2) around to first marker, P2, K 12 tbl, (P2, K2) around to last st, P1.

Rnds 5-13: Repeat Rnds 1-4 twice, then repeat Rnd 1 once **more**.

Bind all sts **loosely** in pattern, working K2 tog 6 times over the 12 sts of the cables before binding them off to reduce flaring of those sts.

Weave side seams ***(Fig. 15, page 76)***.

Design by Mary Marik.

ADULT V-NECK CARDIGAN

INTERMEDIATE

Size	Finished Chest Measurement
Small	35" (89 cm)
Medium	38" (96.5 cm)
Large	41" (104 cm)

Size Note: Instructions are written for size Small with sizes Medium and Large in braces { }. Instructions will be easier to read if you circle all the numbers pertaining to your size. If only one number is given, it applies to all sizes.

MATERIALS

Medium Weight Yarn
[3.5 ounces, 207 yards (100 grams, 188 meters) per ball]:
7{7-8} balls
Straight knitting needles, sizes 6 (4 mm) **and** 8 (5 mm) **or** sizes needed for gauge
Cable needle
Markers
Yarn needle
$^5/_8$" (16 mm) Buttons - 3

GAUGE: With larger size needles, in Stockinette Stitch, 18 sts and 24 rows = 4" (10 cm)

STITCH GUIDE

RIGHT TWIST *(abbreviated RT)* (uses 2 sts)

Knit into the **front** of the second st on the left needle, then knit the first st ***(Figs. 12a & b, page 75)***, letting both sts drop off the needle at the same time.

CABLE 4 FRONT *(abbreviated C4F)* (uses 4 sts)

Slip 2 sts onto cable needle and hold in **front** of work, K2 from left needle, K2 from cable needle.

KEY

- Purl wrong side
- Knit right side
- Knit wrong side
- Purl right side
- K2 tog, YO
- Right Twist
- Cable 4 Front

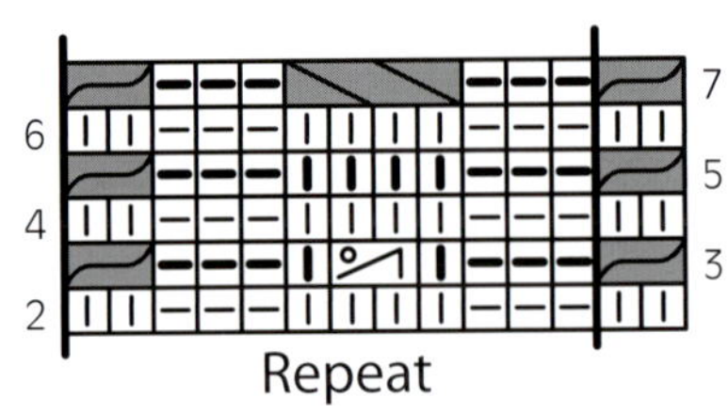

Instructions begin on page 46.

BACK
RIBBING
With smaller size needles, cast on 91{101-111} sts.

Row 1: K1, (P1, K1) across.

Row 2: P1, (K1, P1) across.

Repeat Rows 1 and 2 until Ribbing measures 2½" (6.5 cm), ending by working Row 2.

Increase Row: Work across in established ribbing increasing 25{25-29} sts evenly spaced ***(Figs. 2a & b, page 71)***: 116{126-140} sts.

BODY
Change to larger size needles.

Row 1 (Right side)**:** P3{8-3}, RT ***(Figs. 12a & b, page 75)***, ★ P3, C4F, P3, RT; repeat from ★ 8{8-10} times **more**, P3{8-3}.

Row 2 AND ALL WRONG SIDE ROWS: K3{8-3}, P2, ★ K3, P4, K3, P2; repeat from ★ 8{8-10} times **more**, K3{8-3}.

Row 3: P3{8-3}, RT, ★ P3, K1, K2 tog ***(Fig. 8, page 73)***, YO ***(Fig. 7a, page 72)***, K1, P3, RT; repeat from ★ 8{8-10} times **more**, P3{8-3}.

Row 5: P3{8-3}, RT, ★ P3, K4, P3, RT; repeat from ★ 8{8-10} times **more**, P3{8-3}.

Row 7: P3{8-3}, RT, ★ P3, C4F, P3, RT; repeat from ★ 8{8-10} times **more**, P3{8-3}.

Repeat Rows 2-7 for pattern until Back measures 23{23½-24}"/58.5{59.5-61} cm from cast on edge, ending by working a **wrong** side row.

NECK SHAPING
Maintain established pattern throughout.

Row 1: Work across 37{41-47} sts, bind off next 42{44-46} sts, work across: 37{41-47} sts **each** side.

Both sides of Neck are worked at the same time, using separate yarn for **each** side.

Row 2: Work across; with second yarn, work across.

Row 3 (Decrease row)**:** Work across to within 2 sts of Neck edge, decrease ***(see Decreases, pages 73 and 74)***; with second yarn, decrease, work across: 36{40-46} sts **each** side.

Rows 4 and 5: Repeat Rows 2 and 3: 35{39-45} sts **each** side.

Bind off remaining sts.

LEFT FRONT
RIBBING
With smaller size needles, cast on 49{53-59} sts.

Row 1: K1, (P1, K1) across.

Row 2: P1, (K1, P1) across to last 6 sts, place marker ***(see Markers, page 70)***, **[**(K1, P1) twice, K2 (Band)**]**.

Row 3: K1, (P1, K1) across.

Row 4: P1, (K1, P1) across to last 2 sts, K2.

Repeat Rows 3 and 4 until Ribbing measures 2½" (6.5 cm), ending by working Row 4.

Increase Row: (K1, P1) 3 times, work across in established ribbing increasing 12{13-14} sts evenly spaced: 61{66-73} sts.

BODY

Change to larger size needles.

Row 1 (Right side)**:** P3{8-3}, RT, ★ P3, C4F, P3, RT; repeat from ★ 3{3-4} times **more**, P2, (K1, P1) twice, K2.

Row 2 AND ALL WRONG SIDE ROWS: (K1, P1) 3 times, K2, P2, ★ K3, P4, K3, P2; repeat from ★ 3{3-4} times **more**, K3{8-3}.

Row 3: P3{8-3}, RT, ★ P3, K1, K2 tog, YO, K1, P3, RT; repeat from ★ 3{3-4} times **more**, P2, (K1, P1) twice, K2.

Row 5: P3{8-3}, RT, ★ P3, K4, P3, RT; repeat from ★ 3{3-4} times **more**, P2, (K1, P1) twice, K2.

Row 7: P3{8-3}, RT, ★ P3, C4F, P3, RT; repeat from ★ 3{3-4} times **more**, P2, (K1, P1) twice, K2.

Repeat Rows 2-7 for pattern until Left Front measures 8$\frac{1}{2}$\{9-9$\frac{1}{2}$\}"/21.5{23-24} cm from cast on edge, ending by working a **wrong** side row.

NECK SHAPING

Maintain established pattern throughout.

Row 1 (Decrease row)**:** Work across to within 2 sts of marker, P2 tog ***(Fig. 11, page 74)***, work across: 60{65-72} sts.

Loop a short piece of yarn around last st worked on Row 1 to mark beginning of Neck Shaping.

Row 2: Work across to marker, K1, work across.

Continue to decrease one stitch at Neck edge in same manner, every other row, 0{2-4} times **more *(see Zeros, page 70)***; then decrease every fourth row, 19{18-17} times: 41{45-51} sts.

Work even until Left Front measures same as Back, ending by working a **wrong** side row.

NECKBAND

Bind off 35{39-45} sts removing marker, work across: 6 sts.

Work even until Neckband measures 3{3$\frac{1}{4}$-3$\frac{1}{2}$}"/7.5{8.5-9} cm.

Bind off all sts in pattern.

Mark Front Band for 3 buttons, placing first button $\frac{1}{2}$" (12 mm) above cast on edge and last button $\frac{1}{2}$" (12 mm) below beginning of Neck Shaping; center remaining button.

Instructions continued on page 48.

RIGHT FRONT

RIBBING

With smaller size needles, cast on 49{53-59} sts.

Row 1: K1, (P1, K1) across.

Row 2: [K2, (P1, K1) twice (Band)], place marker, P1, (K1, P1) across.

Row 3: K1, (P1, K1) across.

Row 4 (Buttonhole row)**:** K2, P1, [YO ***(Fig. 7b, page 72)***, P2 tog **(Buttonhole made)**] (K1, P1) across.

Work remaining Buttonholes to match button placement on Left Front.

Row 5: K1, (P1, K1) across.

Row 6: K2, P1, (K1, P1) across.

Repeat Rows 5 and 6 until Ribbing measures 2½" (6.5 cm), ending by working Row 6.

Increase Row: Work across in established ribbing to marker increasing 12{13-14} sts evenly spaced, (P1, K1) 3 times: 61{66-73} sts.

BODY

Change to larger size needles.

Row 1 (Right side)**:** K2, (P1, K1) twice, P2, RT, ★ P3, C4F, P3, RT; repeat from ★ 3{3-4} times **more**, P3{8-3}.

Row 2 AND ALL WRONG SIDE ROWS: K3{8-3}, P2, ★ K3, P4, K3, P2; repeat from ★ 3{3-4} times **more**, K2, (P1, K1) 3 times.

Row 3: K2, (P1, K1) twice, P2, RT, ★ P3, K1, K2 tog, YO, K1, P3, RT; repeat from ★ 3{3-4} times **more**, P3{8-3}.

Row 5: K2, (P1, K1) twice, P2, RT, ★ P3, K4, P3, RT; repeat from ★ 3{3-4} times **more**, P3{8-3}.

Row 7: K2, (P1, K1) twice, P2, RT, ★ P3, C4F, P3, RT; repeat from ★ 3{3-4} times **more**, P3{8-3}.

Repeat Rows 2-7 for pattern until Right Front measures same as Left Front to Neck Shaping, ending by working a **wrong** side row.

NECK SHAPING

Maintain established pattern throughout.

Row 1 (Decrease row)**:** Work across to marker, P2 tog, work across: 60{65-72} sts.

Row 2: Work across to within one st of marker, K1, work across.

Continue to decrease one stitch at Neck edge in same manner, every other row, 0{2-4} times **more**; then decrease every fourth row, 19{18-17} times: 41{45-51} sts.

Work even until Right Front measures same as Left Front to Neckband, ending by working a **right** side row.

NECKBAND

Bind off 35{39-45} sts, work across: 6 sts.

Work even until Neckband measures 3{3 1/4-3 1/2}"/7.5{8.5-9} cm.

Bind off all sts in ribbing.

Sew shoulder seams.

Sew Neckbands together and then sew Neckband to Back Neck edge.

SLEEVE

BODY

Place a marker on **each** side of Front and Back, 8 1/2{9-9 1/2}"/21.5{23-24} cm down from shoulder seam.

With **right** side facing and larger size needles, pick up 100{104-112} sts evenly spaced between markers ***(Fig. 14b, page 76)***.

Row 1 AND ALL WRONG SIDE ROWS: K1{3-1}, P2, ★ K3, P4, K3, P2; repeat from ★ across to last 1{3-1} st(s), K1{3-1}.

Row 2 (Right side)**:** P1{3-1}, RT, ★ P3, C4F, P3, RT; repeat from ★ across to last 1{3-1} st(s), P1{3-1}.

Row 4: P1{3-1}, RT, ★ P3, K1, K2 tog, YO, K1, P3, RT; repeat from ★ across to last 1{3-1} st(s), P1{3-1}.

Row 6: P1{3-1}, RT, ★ P3, K4, P3, RT; repeat from ★ across to last 1{3-1} st(s), P1{3-1}.

Row 8 (Decrease row)**:** Decrease, work across in established pattern to last 2 sts, decrease: 98{102-110} sts.

Maintaining established pattern (Rows 1-6), continue to decrease one stitch at **each** edge, every fourth row, 16{17-19} times **more**: 66{68-72} sts.

Work even until Sleeve measures 17{17 1/2-18}"/43{44.5-45.5} cm **or to desired length** (before Ribbing), ending by working a **right** side row.

RIBBING

Change to smaller size needles.

Decrease Row: Work across in K1, P1 ribbing decreasing 24{24-26} sts evenly spaced: 42{44-46} sts.

Work in K1, P1 ribbing for 2 1/2" (6.5 cm).

Bind off all sts **loosely** in ribbing.

Repeat for second Sleeve.

FINISHING

Weave underarm and side in one continuous seam ***(Fig. 15, page 76)***.

Sew buttons to Band opposite buttonholes.

Design by Carole Prior.

ADULT RAGLAN CARDIGAN

INTERMEDIATE

Size	Finished Chest Measurement
32	36" (91.5 cm)
34	38" (96.5 cm)
36	40" (101.5 cm)
38	42" (106.5 cm)
40	44" (112 cm)
42	46" (117 cm)

Size Note: Instructions are written with sizes 32, 34, and 36 in the first set of braces { } and sizes 38, 40, and 42 in the second set of braces. Instructions will be easier to read if you circle all the numbers pertaining to your size. If only one number is given, it applies to all sizes.

MATERIALS

MEDIUM 4

- Medium Weight Yarn
  - [3.5 ounces, 207 yards (100 grams, 188 meters) per ball]: {7-8-9}{9-10-11} balls
- Straight knitting needles, sizes 5 (3.75 mm) **and** 7 (4.5 mm) **or** sizes needed for gauge
- 16" (40.5 cm) Circular knitting needle, size 5 (3.75 mm)
- Cable needle
- Stitch holders - 7
- Markers
- Yarn needle
- $^3/_4$" (19 mm) Buttons - 6

GAUGE: With larger size needles, in Seed Stitch, 16 sts and 28 rows = 4" (10 cm)

Instructions begin on page 5

STITCH GUIDE

SLIP ST PANEL (uses 10 sts)

RIGHT SLIP *(abbreviated RS)*
(uses 2 sts)
Slip next st onto cable needle and hold in **back** of work, slip 1 from left needle as if to **purl**, K1 from cable needle

LEFT SLIP *(abbreviated LS)*
(uses 2 sts)
Slip next st onto cable needle and hold in **front** of work, K1 from left needle, slip st from cable needle onto right needle.

Row 1 AND ALL WRONG SIDE ROWS: Purl across.
Row 2 (Right side)**:** K3, RS, LS, K3.
Row 4: K2, RS, K2, LS, K2.
Row 6: K1, RS, K4, LS, K1.
Row 8: RS, K6, LS.
Repeat Rows 1-8 for pattern.

DIAMOND PANEL (uses 19 sts)

POPCORN
[K, K tbl *(Fig. 1, page 70)*, K, K tbl, K] **all** in next st.

TWIST 3 BACK *(abbreviated T3B)*
(uses 3 sts)
Slip next st onto cable needle and hold in **back** of work, K2 from left needle, P1 from cable needle.

TWIST 3 FRONT *(abbreviated T3F)*
(uses 3 sts)
Slip 2 sts onto cable needle and hold in **front** of work, P1 from left needle, K2 from cable needle.

TWIST 5 FRONT *(abbreviated T5F)*
(uses 5 sts)
Slip 3 sts onto cable needle and hold in **front** of work, K2 from left needle, slip last st from cable needle onto left needle and purl it, K2 from cable needle.

Row 1: K3, work Popcorn, K3, P2, K1, P2, K3, work Popcorn, K3: 27 sts.
Row 2 (Right side)**:** P3, K5 tog tbl ***(Fig. A)***, P3, T5F, P3, K5 tog tbl, P3: 19 sts.

Fig. A

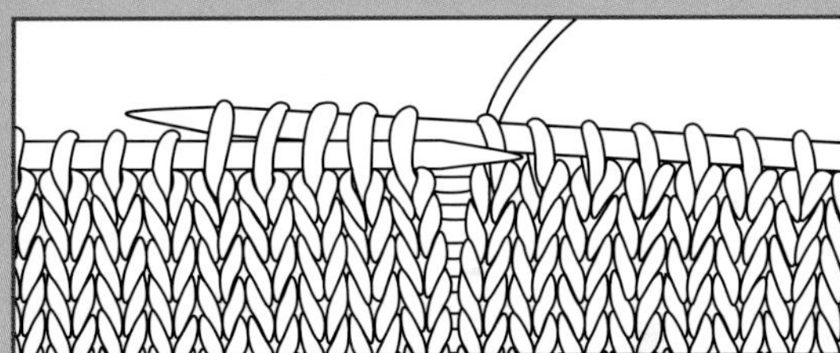

Row 3: K7, P2, K1, P2, K7.
Row 4: P6, T3B, P1, T3F, P6.
Row 5: K6, P2, K3, P2, K6.
Row 6: P5, T3B, P3, T3F, P5.
Row 7: K5, P2, K2, work Popcorn, K2, P2, K5: 23 sts.
Row 8: P4, T3B, P2, K5 tog tbl, P2, T3F, P4: 19 sts.
Row 9: K4, P2, K7, P2, K4.
Row 10: P3, T3B, P7, T3F, P3.
Row 11: K3, P2, K2, work Popcorn, K3, work Popcorn, K2, P2, K3: 27 sts.
Row 12: P2, T3B, P2, K5 tog tbl, P3, K5 tog tbl, P2, T3F, P2: 19 sts.

Stitch Guide continued on page 52.

Row 13: K2, P2, K 11, P2, K2.
Row 14: P2, K2, P 11, K2, P2.
Row 15: K2, P2, K3, (work Popcorn, K3) twice, P2, K2: 27 sts.
Row 16: P2, T3F, P2, K5 tog tbl, P3, K5 tog tbl, P2, T3B, P2: 19 sts.
Row 17: K3, P2, K9, P2, K3.
Row 18: P3, T3F, P7, T3B, P3.
Row 19: K4, P2, K3, work Popcorn, K3, P2, K4: 23 sts.
Row 20: P4, T3F, P2, K5 tog tbl, P2, T3B, P4: 19 sts.
Row 21: K5, (P2, K5) twice.
Row 22: P5, T3F, P3, T3B, P5.
Row 23: K6, P2, K3, P2, K6.
Row 24: P6, T3F, P1, T3B, P6.
Repeat Rows 1-24 for pattern.

HONEYCOMB (Multiple of 4 sts)
Row 1: Purl across.
Row 2 (Right side)**:** ★ Slip next st onto cable needle and hold in **back** of work, K1 from left needle, K1 from cable needle **(Right Twist made)**, slip next st onto cable needle and hold in **front** of work, K1 from left needle, K1 from cable needle **(Left Twist made)**; repeat from ★ across.
Row 3: Purl across.
Row 4: Work (Left Twist, Right Twist) across.
Repeat Rows 1-4 for pattern.

KEY

- Purl wrong side
- Knit right side
- Knit wrong side
- Purl wrong side
- Popcorn
- Left Twist
- Right Twist
- Left Slip
- Right Slip
- Twist 3 Front
- Twist 3 Back
- Twist 5 Front

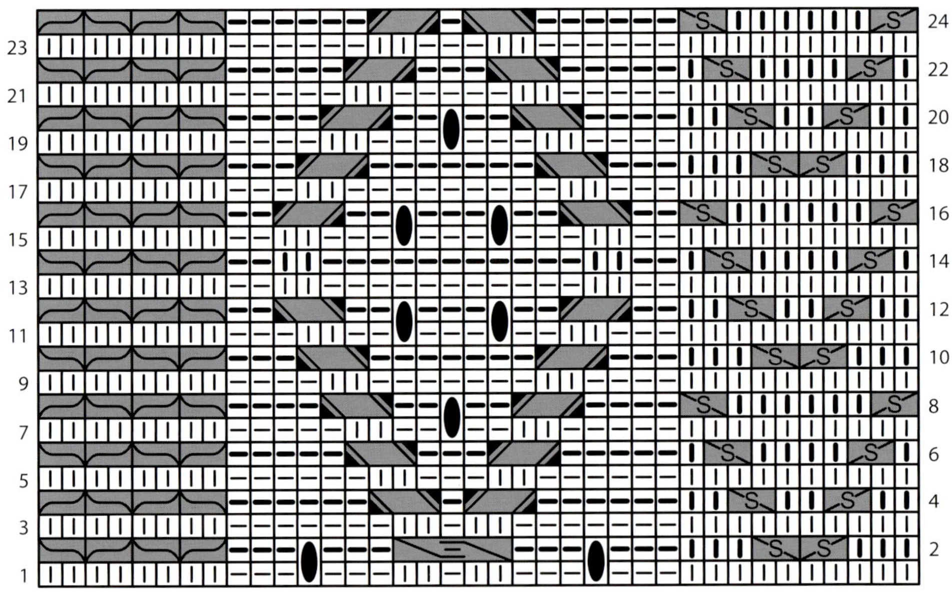

Instructions begin on page 54.

The stitch counts given are based on 19 sts for the Diamond. Add 4 sts to the stitch count for each Bobble being worked.

BACK

TWISTED RIBBING

With smaller size needles, cast on {105-109-113}{117-125-129} sts.

Row 1: P1, **[**K1 tbl ***(Fig. 1, page 70)***, P1**]** across.

Row 2 (Right side)**:** K1 tbl, (P1, K1 tbl) across.

Rows 3-14: Repeat Rows 1 and 2, 6 times increasing one st in center of last row ***(Figs. 2a & b, page 71)***: {106-110-114}{118-126-130} sts.

BODY

Change to larger size needles.

Row 1: (P1, K1) {4-5-6}{7-7-8} times, place marker ***(see Markers, page 70)***, work Row 1 of Slip St Panel, place marker, work Row 1 of Diamond, place marker, work Row 1 of Honeycomb across {32-32-32}{32-40-40} sts, place marker, work Row 1 of Diamond, place marker, work Row 1 of Slip St Panel, place marker, (K1, P1) across.

Row 2 (Right side)**:** K2, (P1, K1) across to next marker, work next row of Slip St Panel, work next row of Diamond, work next row of Honeycomb across to next marker, work next row of Diamond, work next row of Slip St Panel, (K1, P1) across to last 2 sts, K2.

Row 3: (P1, K1) across to next marker, work next row of Slip St Panel, work next row of Diamond, work next row of Honeycomb across to next marker, work next row of Diamond, work next row of Slip St Panel, (K1, P1) across.

Repeat Rows 2 and 3 for pattern until Back measures {19-19-20}{20-21-21}"/ {48.5-48.5-51} {51-53.5-53.5} cm from cast on edge, ending by working a **wrong** side row.

RAGLAN SHAPING

Maintain established pattern throughout.

Rows 1 and 2: Bind off {7-7-7}{7-9-9} sts at the beginning of the next 2 rows, work across: {92-96-100}{104-108-112} sts.

Row 3 (Decrease row)**:** K1, **[**slip 1 as if to **knit**, K1, PSSO ***(Figs. 10a & b, page 74)*****]**, work across to last 3 sts, K2 tog ***(Fig. 8, page 73)***, K1: {90-94-98}{102-106-110} sts.

Row 4: P2, work across to last 2 sts, P2.

Rows 5 thru {56-58-60}{62-64-66}: Repeat Rows 3 and 4, {26-27-28}{29-30-31} times: {38-40-42}{44-46-48} sts.

Slip remaining sts onto st holder; cut yarn.

LEFT FRONT

TWISTED RIBBING

With smaller size needles, cast on {57-59-61} {63-67-69} sts.

Row 1: P1, (K1 tbl, P1) across.

Row 2 (Right side)**:** K1 tbl, (P1, K1 tbl) across.

Rows 3-14: Repeat Rows 1 and 2, 6 times increasing one stitch in center of last row: {58-60-62}{64-68-70} sts.

BODY

Change to larger size needles.

Row 1: P1, (K1 tbl, P1) 4 times, slip 9 sts just worked onto st holder (Band), work Row 1 of Honeycomb across {12-12-12}{12-16-16} sts, place marker, work Row 1 of Diamond, place marker, work Row 1 of Slip St Panel, place marker, (K1, P1) across: {49-51-53}{55-59-61} sts.

Row 2 (Right side)**:** K2, (P1, K1) across to next marker, work next row of Slip St Panel, work next row of Diamond, work next row of Honeycomb across.

Row 3: Work next row of Honeycomb across to next marker, work next row of Diamond, work next row of Slip St Panel, (K1, P1) across.

Repeat Rows 2 and 3 for pattern until Left Front measures same as Back to Raglan Shaping, ending by working a **wrong** side row.

RAGLAN SHAPING

Maintain established pattern throughout.

Row 1: Bind off {7-7-7}{7-9-9} sts, work across: {42-44-46}{48-50-52} sts.

Row 2: Work across to last 2 sts, P2.

Row 3 (Decrease row)**:** K1, slip 1 as if to **knit**, K1, PSSO, work across: {41-43-45}{47-49-51} sts.

Row 4: Work across to last 2 sts, P2.

Instructions continued on page 56.

Rows 5 thru {35-37-39}{41-43-45}: Repeat Rows 3 and 4, {15-16-17}{18-19-20} times; then repeat Row 3 once **more**: {25-26-27} {28-29-30} sts.

NECK SHAPING

Row 1: Work across {7-8-9}{10-11-12} sts, slip sts just worked onto st holder, work across to last 2 sts, P2: 18 sts.

Row 2 (Decrease row)**:** K1, slip 1 as if to **knit**, K1, PSSO, work across to last 2 sts, K2 tog: 16 sts.

Row 3 (Decrease row)**:** P2 tog ***(Fig. 11, page 74)***, work across to last 2 sts, P2: 15 sts.

Row 4 (Decrease row)**:** K1, slip 1 as if to **knit**, K1, PSSO, work across to last 2 sts, K2 tog: 13 sts.

Row 5: Work across to last 2 sts, P2.

Rows 6-13: Repeat Rows 4 and 5, 4 times: 5 sts.

Row 14 (Decrease row)**:** K1, slip 1 as if to **knit**, K1, PSSO, work across: 4 sts.

Row 15: Work across to last 2 sts, P2.

Rows 16 and 17: Repeat Rows 14 and 15: 3 sts.

Row 18: K1, slip 1 as if to **knit**, K1, PSSO: 2 sts.

Row 19: P2.

Row 20: K2 tog, cut yarn and pull through st.

RIGHT FRONT

TWISTED RIBBING

Work same as Left Front, page 50, through Row 5.

Row 6 (Buttonhole row)**:** K1 tbl, P1, K1 tbl, bind off next 2 sts, K1 tbl, (P1, K1 tbl) across: {55-57-59}{61-65-67} sts.

Row 7: (P1, K1 tbl) across to bound off sts, **turn**; add on 2 sts ***(Figs. 6a & b, page 72)***, **turn**; P1, K1 tbl, P1: {57-59-61}{63-67-69} sts.

Row 8: Repeat Row 2.

Rows 9-14: Repeat Rows 1 and 2, 3 times increasing one stitch in center of last row: {58-60-62}{64-68-70} sts.

BODY

Change to larger size needles.

Row 1: (P1, K1) {4-5-6}{7-7-8} times, place marker, work Row 1 of Slip St Panel, place marker, work Row 1 of Diamond, place marker, work Row 1 of Honeycomb across {12-12-12}{12-16-16} sts, slip remaining 9 sts onto st holder (Band): {49-51-53}{55-59-61} sts.

Row 2 (Right side)**:** Work next row of Honeycomb across to next marker, work next row of Diamond, work next row of Slip St Panel, (K1, P1) across to last 2 sts, K2.

Row 3: (P1, K1) across to next marker, work next row of Slip St Panel, work next row of Diamond, work next row of Honeycomb across.

Repeat Rows 2 and 3 for pattern until Right Front measures same as Back to Raglan Shaping, ending by working a **right** side row.

RAGLAN SHAPING
Maintain established pattern throughout.

Row 1: Bind off {7-7-7}{7-9-9} sts, work across: {42-44-46}{48-50-52} sts.

Row 2 (Decrease row)**:** Work across to last 3 sts, K2 tog, K1: {41-43-45}{47-49-51} sts.

Row 3: P2, work across.

Rows 4 thru {35-37-39}{41-43-45}: Repeat Rows 2 and 3, {16-17-18}{19-20-21} times: {25-26-27}{28-29-30} sts.

NECK SHAPING
Row 1: Work across {7-8-9}{10-11-12} sts, slip sts just worked onto st holder, work across to last 3 sts, K2 tog, K1: 17 sts.

Row 2 (Decrease row)**:** P2, work across to last 2 sts, P2 tog: 16 sts.

Row 3 (Decrease row)**:** Slip 1 as if to **knit**, K1, PSSO, work across to last 3 sts, K2 tog, K1: 14 sts.

Row 4 (Decrease row)**:** P2, work across to last 2 sts, P2 tog: 13 sts.

Row 5 (Decrease row)**:** Work across to last 3 sts, K2 tog, K1: 12 sts.

Rows 6-13: Repeat Rows 4 and 5, 4 times: 4 sts.

Row 14: P2, work across.

Row 15: K1, K2 tog, K1: 3 sts.

Row 16: Purl across.

Row 17: K1, K2 tog: 2 sts.

Row 18: P2.

Row 19: K2 tog, cut yarn and pull through st.

SLEEVE (Make 2)

TWISTED RIBBING
With smaller size needles, cast on {41-43-45}{47-49-51} sts.

Row 1: P1, (K1 tbl, P1) across.

Row 2 (Right side)**:** K1 tbl, (P1, K1 tbl) across.

Repeat Rows 1 and 2, {6-6-7}{7-8-8} times increasing {10-12-10}{12-10-12} sts evenly spaced across last row: {51-55-55}{59-59-63} sts.

BODY
Change to larger size needles.

Row 1: (P1, K1) {3-4-4}{5-5-6} times, place marker, work Row 1 of Slip St Panel, place marker, work Row 1 of Diamond, place marker, work Row 1 of Slip St Panel, place marker, (K1, P1) across.

Row 2 (Right side)**:** K2, (P1, K1) across to next marker, work next row of Slip St Panel, work next row of Diamond, work next row of Slip St Panel, (K1, P1) across to last 2 sts, K2.

Row 3: (P1, K1) across to next marker, work next row of Slip St Panel, work next row of Diamond, work next row of Slip St Panel, (K1, P1) across.

Instructions continued on page 58.

Maintain the first and last stitch in Stockinette Stitch and work new stitches in Seed Stitch (knit the purl sts and purl the knit sts as they face you).

Repeat Rows 2 and 3 for pattern, increasing one stitch at **each** edge, every {8-8-8}{8-6-6} rows, {6-1-5}{8-1-5} time(s); then increase every {10-10-10}{0-8-8} rows, {1-5-2}{0-8-5} time(s) ***(see Zeros, page 70)***: {65-67-69}{75-77-83} sts.

Work even until Sleeve measures approximately {17 1/2-17 1/2-18}{18-18 1/2-18 1/2}"/{44.5-44.5-45.5}{45.5-47-47} cm from cast on edge **or desired length to Raglan Shaping**, ending by working a **right** side row.

RAGLAN SHAPING

Maintain established pattern throughout.

Rows 1 and 2: Bind off {7-7-7}{7-9-9} sts at the beginning of the next 2 rows, work across: {51-53-55}{61-59-65} sts.

Row 3: P2, work across to last 2 sts, P2.

Row 4: K2, work across to last 2 sts, K2.

Row 5: P2, work across to last 2 sts, P2.

Row 6 (Decrease row)**:** K1, slip 1 as if to **knit**, K1, PSSO, work across to last 3 sts, K2 tog, K1: {49-51-53}{59-57-63} sts.

Repeat Rows 3-6, 3 times: {43-45-47}{53-51-57} sts.

Repeat Rows 5 and 6, {19-20-21}{22-23-24} times: {5-5-5}{9-5-9} sts.

Slip remaining sts onto st holder; cut yarn.

LEFT FRONT BAND

Row 1: With **right** side facing, slip sts from st holder onto smaller size needle; K1 tbl, (P1, K1 tbl) across: 9 sts.

Row 2: P1, (K1 tbl, P1) across.

Row 3: K1 tbl, (P1, K1 tbl) across.

Repeat Rows 2 and 3 until Band (slightly stretched) measures same as Left Front to Neck Shaping, ending by working a **wrong** side row.

Slip sts onto Left Neck st holder; cut yarn.

Weave Band to Front ***(Fig. 15, page 76)***.

Mark Left Front Band for 5 buttons as follows: placing first button to match buttonhole on Right Front Band and, remembering that the last (sixth) button will be placed on Row 1 of the Neck ribbing, space remaining buttons evenly.

RIGHT FRONT BAND

Row 1: With **wrong** side facing, slip sts from st holder onto smaller size needle; P1, (K1 tbl, P1) across: 9 sts.

Row 2: K1 tbl, (P1, K1 tbl) across.

Row 3: P1, (K1 tbl, P1) across.

Repeat Rows 2 and 3, adding buttonholes in same manner as Right Front Twisted Ribbing to correspond with placement of buttons, until Band (slightly stretched) measures same as Right Front to Neck Shaping, ending by working a **wrong** side row.

Slip sts onto Right Neck st holder; cut yarn.

Weave Band to Front.

Weave raglan seams.

Weave underarm and side in one continuous seam.

TWISTED NECK RIBBING

With **right** side facing, using circular needle and beginning with Right Front st holder, work across Right Front Band in established ribbing, knit {7-8-9}{10-11-12} sts, pick up 10 sts evenly spaced along right Neck edge ***(Fig. 14b, page 76)***, slip {5-5-5}{9-5-9} sts from Sleeve st holder onto opposite end and knit across, slip {38-40-42}{44-46-48} sts from Back st holder onto opposite end and knit across, slip {5-5-5}{9-5-9} sts from Sleeve st holder onto opposite end and knit across, pick up 11 sts evenly space along left Neck edge, slip {7-8-9}{10-11-12} sts from Left Front st holder onto opposite end and work across Left Front Band in established ribbing: {101-105-109}{121-117-129} sts.

Row 1: P1, (K1 tbl, P1) across.

Row 2 (Buttonhole row)**:** K1 tbl, P1, K1 tbl, bind off 2 sts, K1 tbl, (P1, K1 tbl) across: {99-103-107}{119-115-127} sts.

Row 3: (P1, K1 tbl) across to bound off sts, **turn**; add on 2 sts, **turn**; P1, K1 tbl, P1: {101-105-109}{121-117-129} sts.

Row 4: K1 tbl, (P1, K1 tbl) across.

Row 5: P1, (K1 tbl, P1) across.

Rows 6 and 7: Repeat Rows 4 and 5.

Bind off all sts **loosely** in ribbing.

Sew buttons to Button Band.

Design by Jeannine C. LaRoche.

AFGHAN

INTERMEDIATE

Finished Size: 44 1/2"w x 65"h (113 cm x 165 cm)

MATERIALS

Super Bulky Weight Yarn (SUPER BULKY 6)
[6 ounces, 143 yards (170 grams, 130 meters) per skein]: 10 skeins
29" (73.5 cm) Circular knitting needle, size 13 (9 mm) **or** size needed for gauge
Cable needle

GAUGE: In Seed Stitch, 10 sts = 4" (10 cm)

STITCH GUIDE

CABLE 6 BACK *(abbreviated C6B)* (uses 6 sts)
Slip 3 sts onto cable needle and hold in **back** of work, K3 from the left needle, K3 from the cable needle.

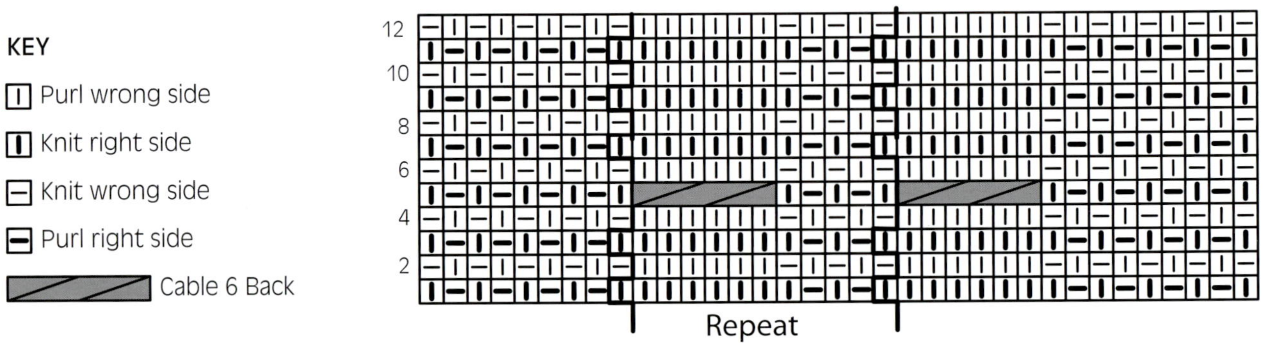

TOP BORDER

Cast on 111 sts.

Row 1: K1, (P1, K1) across.

Repeat Row 1 until Top Border measures 2 1/2" (6.5 cm) from cast on edge.

Increase Row: K1, (P1, K1) 4 times, ★ P6, K1, (P1, K1) twice; repeat from ★ across to last 14 sts, purl increase ***(Fig. 4, page 71)***, P4, K1, (P1, K1) 4 times: 112 sts.

BODY

Row 1 (Right side)**:** (K1, P1) 4 times, K8, ★ (P1, K1) twice, K7; repeat from ★ across to last 8 sts, (P1, K1) 4 times.

Row 2: K1, (P1, K1) 4 times, P6, ★ K1, (P1, K1) twice, P6; repeat from ★ across to last 9 sts, K1, (P1, K1) 4 times.

Rows 3 and 4: Repeat Rows 1 and 2.

Row 5: K1, (P1, K1) 4 times, C6B, ★ K1, (P1, K1) twice, C6B; repeat from ★ across to last 9 sts, K1, (P1, K1) 4 times.

Row 6: K1, (P1, K1) 4 times, P6, ★ K1, (P1, K1) twice, P6; repeat from ★ across to last 9 sts, K1, (P1, K1) 4 times.

Rows 7-12: Repeat Rows 1 and 2, 3 times.

Repeat Rows 1-12 for pattern until Afghan measures 62$^{1}/_{2}$" (159 cm), ending by working Row 9.

BOTTOM BORDER

Row 1: K1, (P1, K1) 4 times, ★ P6, K1, (P1, K1) twice; repeat from ★ across to last 15 sts, P2 tog ***(Fig. 11, page 74)***, P4, K1, (P1, K1) 4 times: 111 sts.

Row 2: K1, (P1, K1) across.

Repeat Row 2 until Bottom Border measures 2$^{1}/_{2}$" (6.5 cm).

Bind off all sts in pattern.

SMALL PILLOW

INTERMEDIATE

Finished Size: 16" (40.5 cm) square

MATERIALS
Medium Weight Yarn
[5 ounces, 256 yards
(140 grams, 234 meters) per ball]: 2 balls
Straight knitting needles, size 8 (5 mm) **or** size needed for gauge
Cable needle
Yarn needle
Pillow form, 16" (40.5 cm) square

GAUGE: In Garter St, 20 sts = 4" (10 cm)

STITCH GUIDE

CABLE 8 FRONT *(abbreviated C8F)* (uses 8 sts)
Slip 4 sts onto cable needle and hold in **front** of work, K4 from left needle, K4 from cable needle.

CABLE 9 FRONT *(abbreviated C9F)* (uses 9 sts)
Slip 4 sts onto cable needle and hold in **front** of work, K5 from left needle, K4 from cable needle.

KEY
Purl wrong side
Knit right side
Knit wrong side
Purl right side
Cable 8 Front
Cable 9 Front

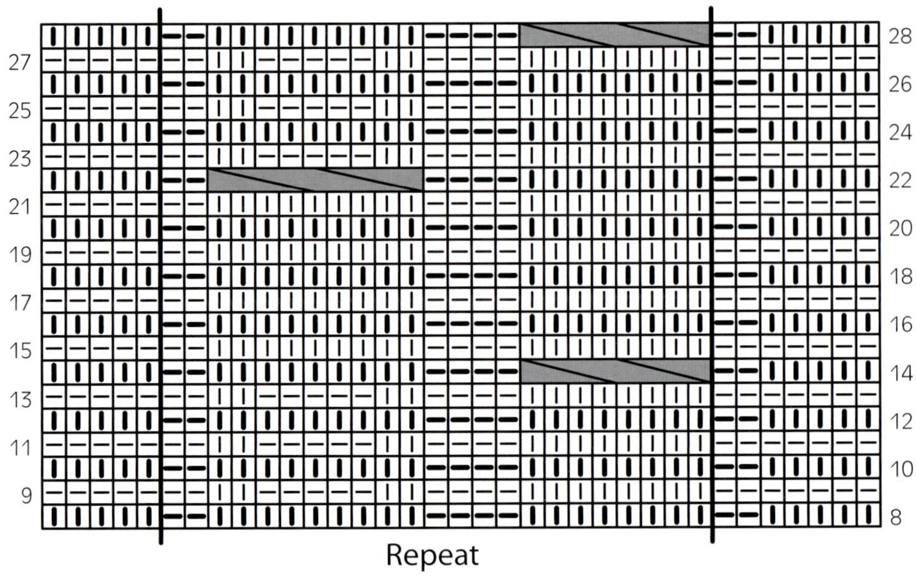

Instructions begin on page 64.

BODY (Make 2)

Cast on 69 sts.

Rows 1-6: Knit across.

Row 7: Knit across increasing 12 sts evenly spaced ***(Figs. 2a & b, page 71)***: 81 sts.

Row 8 (Right side)**:** K5, P2, ★ K8, P4, K9, P2; repeat from ★ 2 times **more**, K5.

Row 9: K7, ★ † P2, K5, P2, K4, P8 †, K2; repeat from ★ once **more**, then repeat from † to † once, K7.

Rows 10-13: Repeat Rows 8 and 9 twice.

Row 14: K5, P2, ★ C8F, P4, K9, P2; repeat from ★ 2 times **more**, K5.

Row 15: K7, ★ † P9, K4, P8 †, K2; repeat from ★ once **more**, then repeat from † to † once, K7.

Row 16: K5, P2, ★ K8, P4, K9, P2; repeat from ★ 2 times **more**, K5.

Rows 17-21: Repeat Rows 15 and 16 twice, then repeat Row 15 once **more**.

Row 22: K5, P2, ★ K8, P4, C9F, P2; repeat from ★ 2 times **more**, K5.

Row 23: Repeat Row 9.

Rows 24-27: Repeat Rows 8 and 9 twice.

Row 28: Repeat Row 14.

Rows 29-89: Repeat Rows 15-28, 4 times; then repeat Rows 15-19 once **more**.

Row 90: Knit across decreasing 12 sts evenly spaced ***(Fig. 8, page 73)***: 69 sts.

Rows 91-95: Knit across.

Bind off all sts in **knit**.

With **wrong** sides together, sew Pillow together, inserting pillow form before closing last side.

Design by Sarah J. Green.

LARGE PILLOW

Shown on page 67.

INTERMEDIATE

Finished Size: 18" (45.5 cm) square

MATERIALS

Medium Weight Yarn (MEDIUM 4)
[5 ounces, 256 yards
(140 grams, 234 meters) per ball]: 2 balls
Straight knitting needles, size 8 (5 mm) **or** size needed for gauge
Cable needle
Yarn needle
Pillow form, 18" (45.5 cm) square

GAUGE: In pattern, 20 sts = 4" (10 cm)

STITCH GUIDE

CABLE 6 FRONT *(abbreviated C6F)* (uses 6 sts)
Slip 3 sts onto cable needle and hold in **front** of work, K3 from left needle, K3 from cable needle.

CABLE 6 BACK *(abbreviated C6B)* (uses 6 sts)
Slip 3 sts onto cable needle and hold in **back** of work, K3 from left needle, K3 from cable needle.

KNIT 1 BELOW *(abbreviated K1B)*
When instructed to K1B, insert needle into st **below** next st on left needle and knit it ***(Fig. A)***, allowing st on needle to fall to the back.

Fig. A

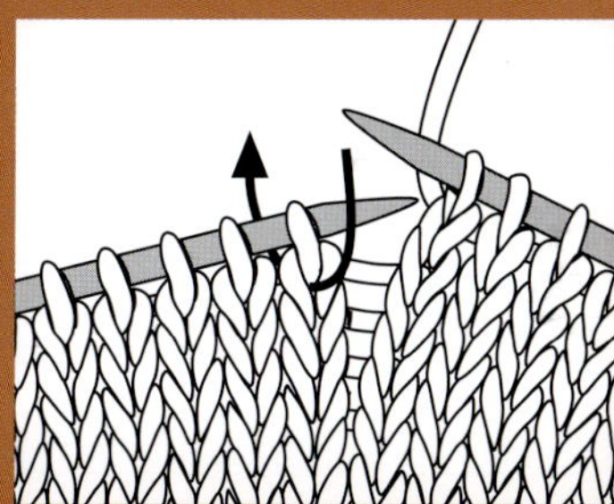

Instructions begin on page 66.

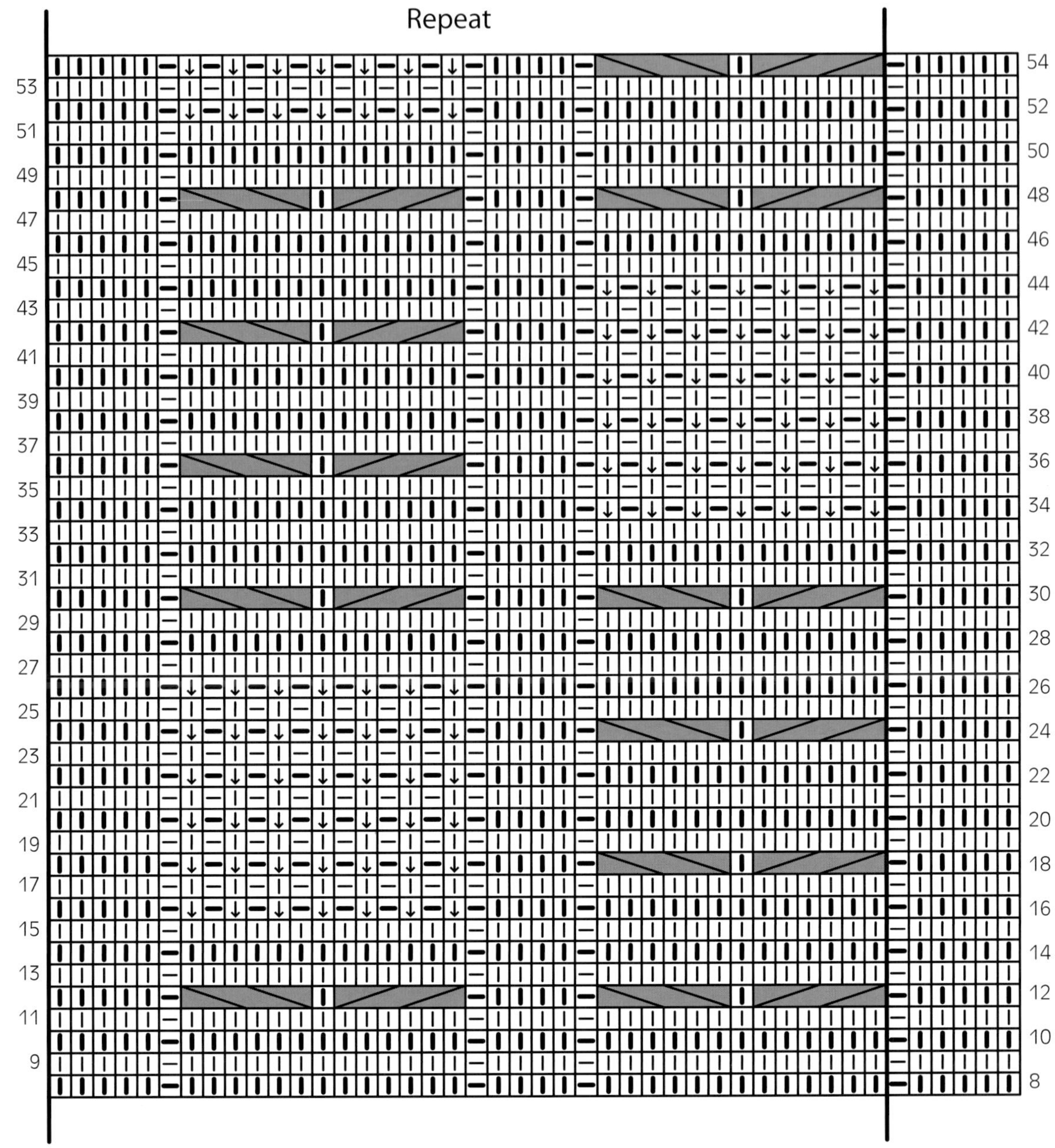

KEY

- Purl wrong side
- Knit right side
- Knit wrong side
- Purl right side
- Knit 1 Below
- Cable 6 Front
- Cable 6 Back

BODY (Make 2)

Cast on 70 sts.

Row 1: Purl across

Row 2 (Right side)**:** Knit across.

Rows 3-5: Repeat Rows 1 and 2 once, then repeat Row 1 once **more**.

Instructions continued on page 68.

Row 6: K7, M1 ***(Figs. 3a & b, page 71)***, (K5, M1) 11 times, K8: 82 sts.

Row 7: Purl across.

Row 8: K5, P1, K 13, P1, ★ K4, P1, K 13, P1; repeat from ★ 2 times **more**, K5.

Row 9: P5, K1, P 13, K1, ★ P4, K1, P 13, K1; repeat from ★ 2 times **more**, P5.

Rows 10 and 11: Repeat Rows 8 and 9.

Row 12: K5, P1, C6B, K1, C6F, P1, ★ K4, P1, C6B, K1, C6F, P1; repeat from ★ 2 times **more**, K5.

Rows 13-15: Repeat Rows 9-11.

Row 16: K5, † P1, K 13, P1, K4, P1, [K1B ***(Fig. A, page 65)***, P1] 7 times †, K4, repeat from † to † once, K5

Row 17: P5, † K1, (P1, K1) 7 times, P4, K1, P 13, K1 †, P4, repeat from † to † once, P5.

Row 18: K5, † P1, C6B, K1, C6F, P1, K4, P1, (K1B, P1) 7 times †, K4, repeat from † to † once, K5.

Row 19: P5, † K1, (P1, K1) 7 times, P4, K1, P 13, K1 †, P4, repeat from † to † once, P5.

Rows 20 and 21: Repeat Rows 16 and 17.

Rows 22-27: Repeat Rows 16-21.

Rows 28 and 29: Repeat Rows 8 and 9.

Rows 30-33: Repeat Rows 12-15.

Row 34: K5, P1, † (K1B, P1) 7 times, K4, P1, K 13, P1 †, repeat from † to † once, K5.

Row 35: P5, K1, † P 13, K1, P4, (K1, P1) 7 times, K1 †, P4, repeat from † to † once, P5.

Row 36: K5, P1, † (K1B, P1) 7 times, K4, P1, C6B, K1, C6F, P1 †, K4, repeat from † to † once, K5.

Row 37: P5, K1, † P 13, K1, P4, (K1, P1) 7 times, K1 †, P4, repeat from † to † once, P5.

Rows 38 and 39: Repeat Rows 34 and 35.

Rows 40-44: Repeat Rows 34-38.

Rows 45-47: Repeat Rows 9-11.

Rows 48-105: Repeat Rows 12-47 once, then repeat Rows 12-33 once **more**.

Row 106: K7, K2 tog ***(Fig. 8, page 73)***, (K4, K2 tog) 11 times, K7: 70 sts.

Row 107: Purl across.

Row 108: Knit across.

Rows 109 and 110: Repeat Rows 107 and 108.

Bind off all sts in **purl**.

With **wrong** sides together, sew Pillow together, inserting pillow form before closing.

Design by Sarah J. Green.

ABBREVIATIONS

C3B	Cable 3 Back
C4B	Cable 4 Back
C6B	Cable 6 Back
C8B	Cable 8 Back
C3F	Cable 3 Front
C4F	Cable 4 Front
C6F	Cable 6 Front
C8F	Cable 8 Front
C9F	Cable 9 Front
cm	centimeters
LS	Left Slip
LT	Left Twist
K	knit
K1B	knit 1 below
M1	make one
M1P	make one purl
mm	millimeters
P	purl
PSSO	pass slipped stitch over
Rnd(s)	Round(s)
RS	Right Slip
RT	Right Twist
SSK	slip, slip, knit
st(s)	stitch(es)
T2B	Twist 2 Back
T3B	Twist 3 Back
T4B	Twist 4 Back
T2F	Twist 2 Front
T3F	Twist 3 FRont
T4F	Twist 4 Front
T5F	Twist 5 Front
tbl	through back loop(s)
tog	together
WYB	with yarn in back
YO	yarn over

GENERAL INSTRUCTIONS

★ — work instructions following ★ as many **more** times as indicated in addition to the first time.

† to † — work all instructions from first † to second † **as many** times as specified.

( ) or **[ ]** — work enclosed instructions **as many** times as specified by the number immediately following **or** work all enclosed instructions in the stitch or space indicated **or** contains explanatory remarks.

colon (:) — the number(s) given after a colon at the end of a row or round denote(s) the number of stitches you should have on that row or round.

work even — work without increasing or decreasing in the established pattern.

GAUGE

Exact gauge is essential for proper size or fit. Before beginning your project, make a sample swatch in the yarn and needle specified. After completing the swatch, measure it, counting your stitches and rows carefully. If your swatch is larger or smaller than specified, **make another, changing needle size to get the correct gauge**. Keep trying until you find the size needles that will give you the specified gauge. Once proper gauge is obtained, measure width of a garment approximately every 3" (7.5 cm) to be sure gauge remains consistent.

If you have more rows per inch than specified, use a larger size needle for the purl rows; if fewer, use a smaller size needle for the purl rows.

ZEROS

To consolidate the length of an involved pattern, zeros are sometimes used so that all sizes can be combined. For example, increase every sixth row 5{1-0} time(s) means the first size would increase 5 times, the second size would increase once, and the largest size would do nothing.

MARKERS

As a convenience to you, we have used markers to help distinguish the beginning of a pattern or a round. Place markers as instructed. You may use purchased markers or tie a length of contrasting color yarn around the needle. When you reach a marker on each row or round, slip it from the left needle to the right needle; remove it when no longer needed.

KNIT TERMINOLOGY		
UNITED STATES		INTERNATIONAL
gauge	=	tension
bind off	=	cast off
yarn over (YO)	=	yarn forward (yfwd) **or** yarn around needle (yrn)

Fig. 1

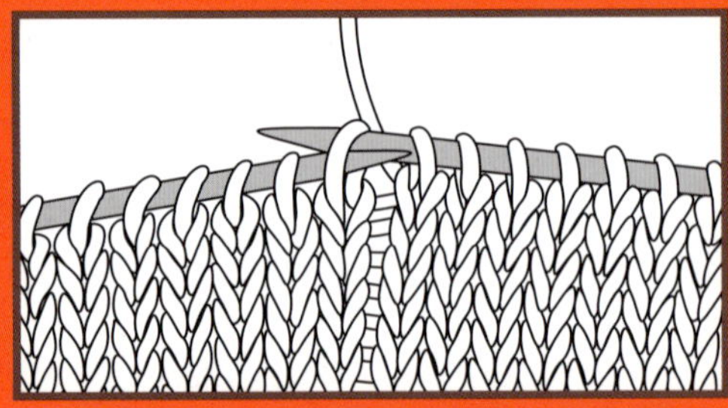

KNIT 1 THROUGH BACK LOOP

(abbreviated K1 tbl)

Insert the right needle through the back loop of the next stitch ***(Fig. 1)*** and knit it.

Yarn Weight Symbol & Names	SUPER FINE 1	FINE 2	LIGHT 3	MEDIUM 4	BULKY 5	SUPER BULKY 6
Type of Yarns in Category	Sock, Fingering Baby	Sport, Baby	DK, Light Worsted	Worsted, Afghan, Aran	Chunky, Craft, Rug	Bulky, Roving
Knit Gauge Ranges in Stockinette St to 4" (10 cm)	27-32 sts	23-26 sts	21-24 sts	16-20 sts	12-15 sts	6-11 sts
Advised Needle Size Range	1-3	3-5	5-7	7-9	9-11	11 and larger

KNITTING NEEDLES																
U.S.	0	1	2	3	4	5	6	7	8	9	10	10½	11	13	15	17
U.K.	13	12	11	10	9	8	7	6	5	4	3	2	1	00	000	---
Metric - mm	2	2.25	2.75	3.25	3.5	3.75	4	4.5	5	5.5	6	6.5	8	9	10	12.75

BEGINNER	Projects for first-time knitters using basic knit and purl stitches. Minimal shaping.
EASY	Projects using basic stitches, repetitive stitch patterns, simple color changes, and simple shaping and finishing.
INTERMEDIATE	Projects with a variety of stitches, such as basic cables and lace, simple intarsia, double-pointed needles and knitting in the round needle techniques, mid-level shaping and finishing.
EXPERIENCED	Projects using advanced techniques and stitches, such as short rows, fair isle, more intricate intarsia, cables, lace patterns, and numerous color changes.

INCREASES

KNIT INCREASE

Knit the next stitch but do **not** slip the old stitch off the left needle ***(Fig. 2a)***. Insert the right needle into the back loop of the same stitch and knit it ***(Fig. 2b)***, then slip the old stitch off the left needle.

MAKE ONE *(abbreviated M1)*

Insert the **left** needle under the horizontal strand between the stitches from the **front** ***(Fig. 3a)***. Then knit into the **back** of the strand ***(Fig. 3b)***.

PURL INCREASE

Purl the next stitch but do **not** slip the old stitch off the left needle. Insert the right needle into the **back** loop of the same stitch from **back** to **front** ***(Fig. 4)*** and purl it. Slip the old stitch off the left needle.

Fig. 2a

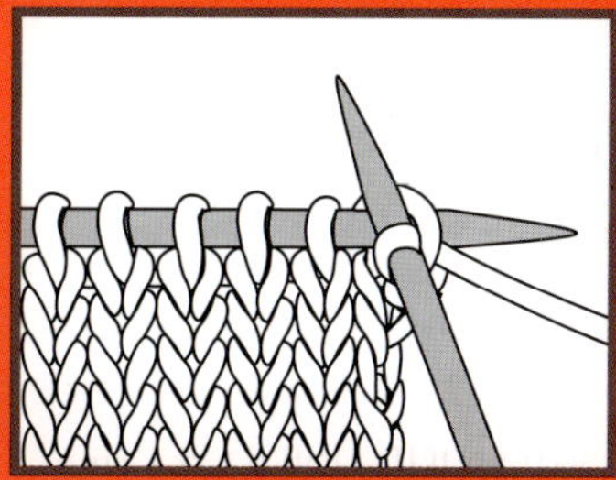

Fig. 2b

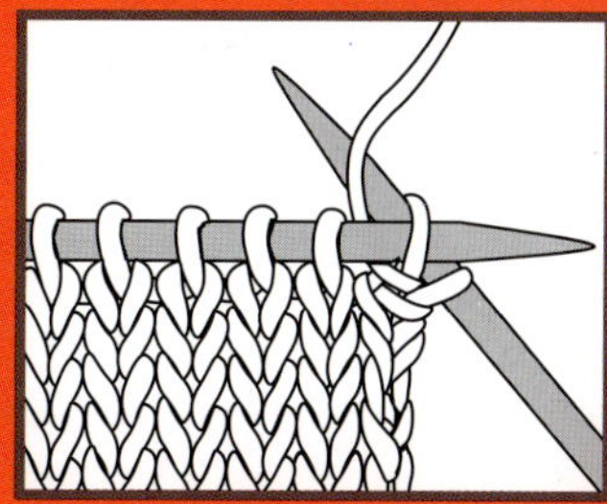

Fig. 3a

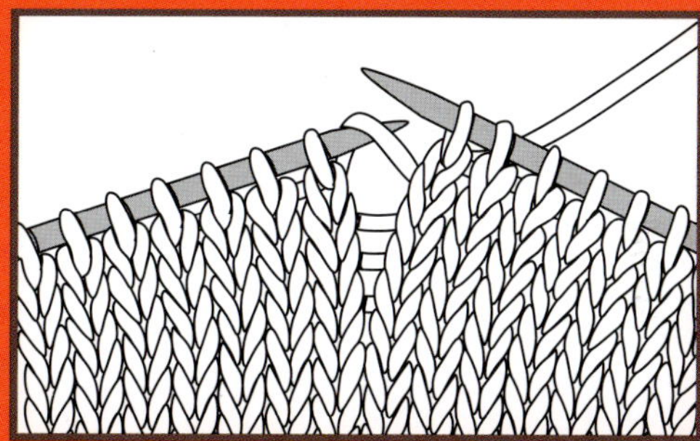

Fig. 3b

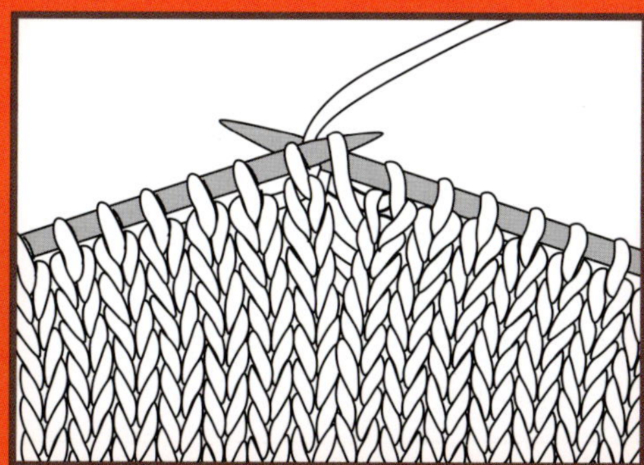

Fig. 4

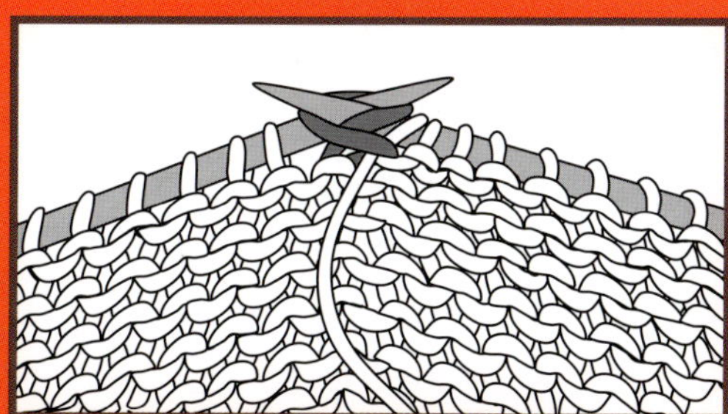

MAKE ONE PURL

(abbreviated M1P)

Insert the **left** needle under the horizontal strand between the stitches from the **back** ***(Fig. 5a)***. Then purl the strand ***(Fig. 5b)***.

Fig. 5a

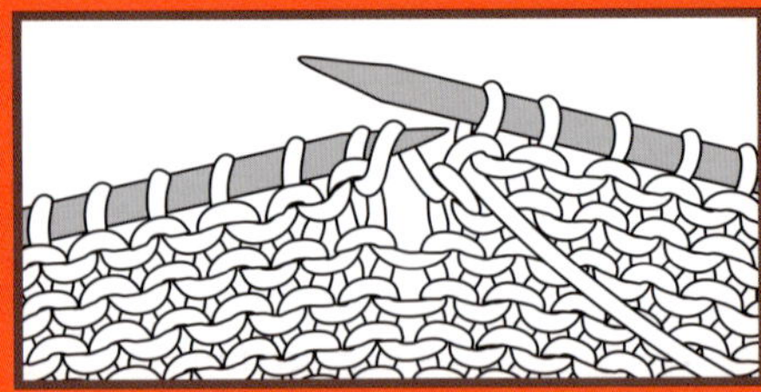

Fig. 5b

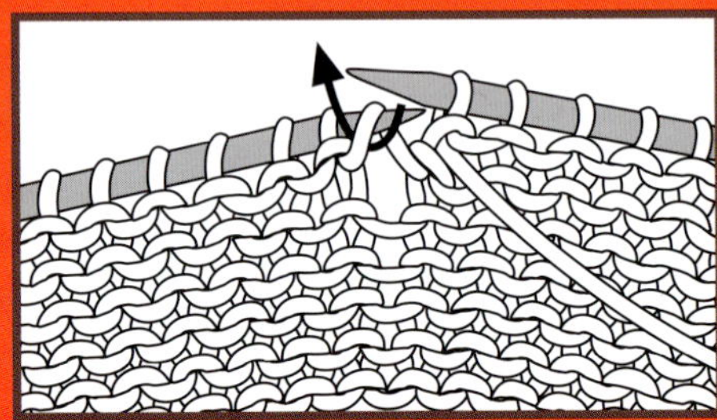

ADDING NEW STITCHES

Insert the right needle into stitch as if to **knit**, yarn over and pull loop through ***(Fig. 6a)***, insert the left needle into the loop just worked from **front** to **back** and slip the loop onto the left needle ***(Fig. 6b)***. Repeat for required number of stitches.

Fig. 6a

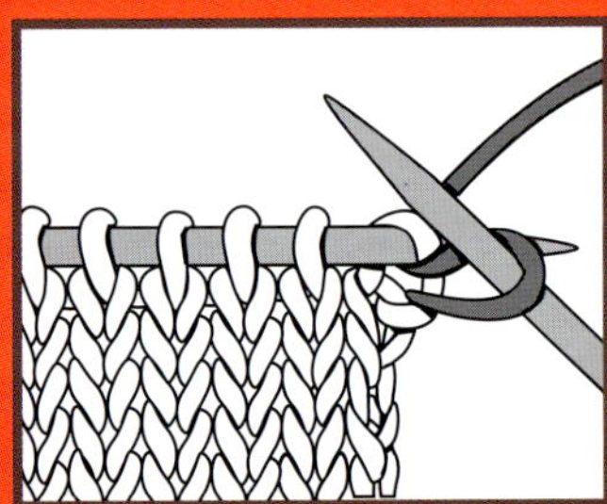

Fig. 6b

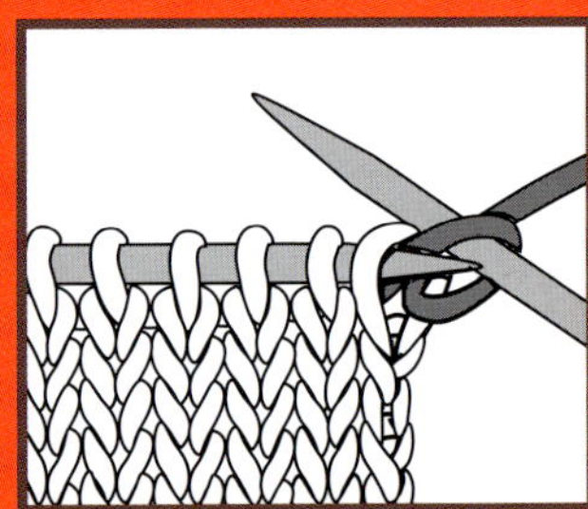

YARN OVERS

After a knit stitch, before a knit stitch

Bring the yarn forward **between** the needles, then back **over** the top of the right hand needle, so that it is now in position to knit the next stitch ***(Fig. 7a)***.

Fig. 7a

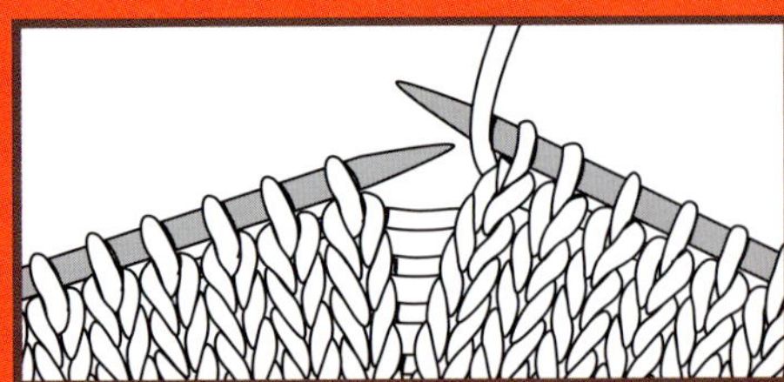

After a purl stitch, before a purl stitch

Take yarn **over** the right hand needle to the back, then forward **under** it, so that it is now in position to purl the next stitch ***(Fig. 7b)***.

Fig. 7b

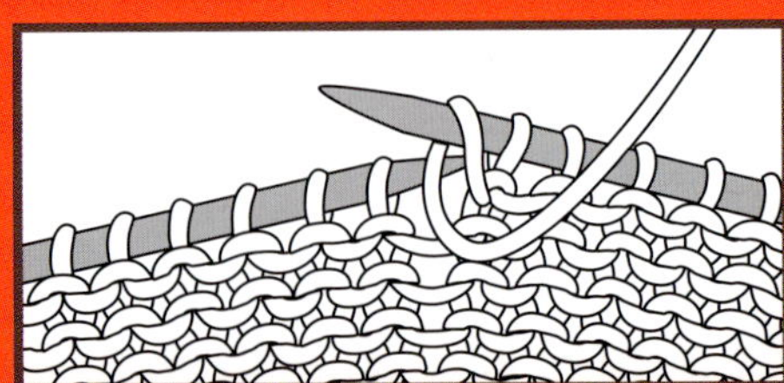

DECREASES

KNIT 2 TOGETHER

(abbreviated K2 tog)

Insert the right needle into the **front** of the first two stitches on the left needle as if to **knit** ***(Fig. 8)***, then **knit** them together as if they were one stitch.

SLIP, SLIP, KNIT *(abbreviated SSK)*

Separately slip two stitches as if to **knit** ***(Fig. 9a)***. Insert the **left** needle into the **front** of both slipped stitches ***(Fig. 9b)*** and knit them together ***(Fig. 9c)***.

Fig. 8

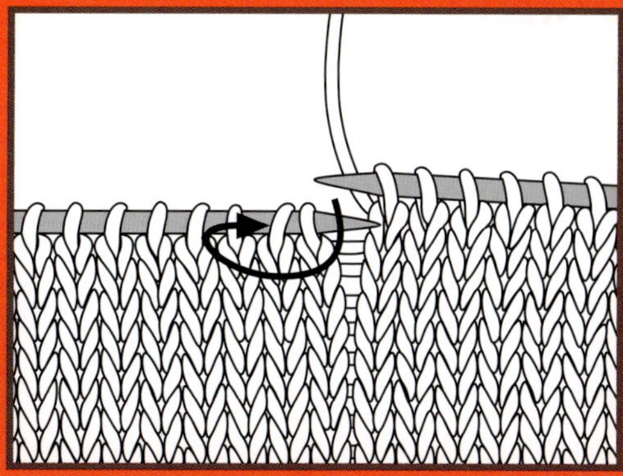

Fig. 9a

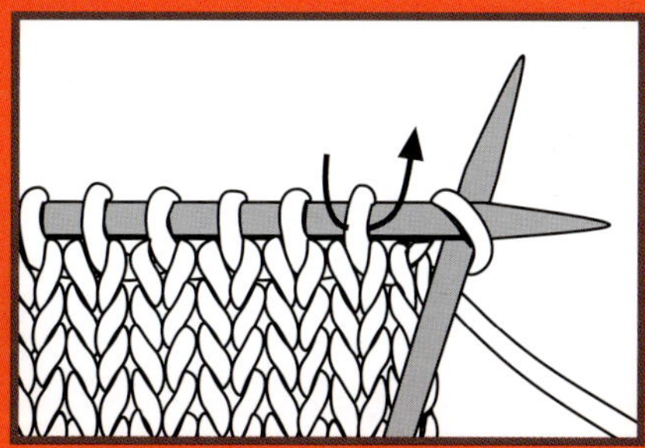

Fig. 9b

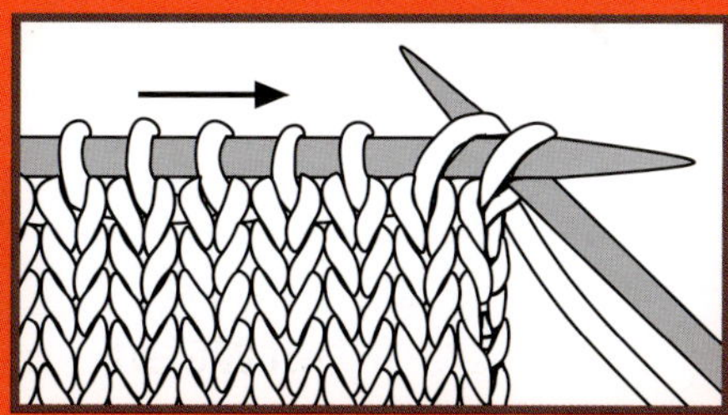

Fig. 9c

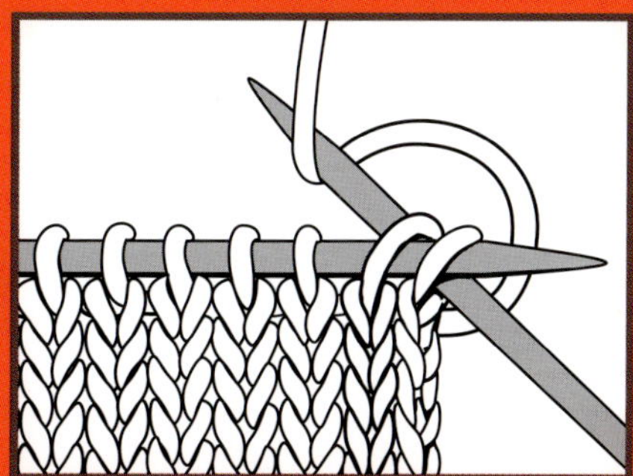

SLIP 1, KNIT 1, PASS SLIPPED STITCH OVER

(abbreviated slip 1, K1, PSSO)

Slip one stitch as if to **knit** ***(Fig. 10a)***. Knit the next stitch. With the left needle, bring the slipped stitch over the knit stitch ***(Fig. 10b)*** and off the needle.

PURL 2 TOGETHER

(abbreviated P2 tog)

Insert the right needle into the **front** of the first two stitches on the left needle as if to **purl** ***(Fig. 11)***, then **purl** them together.

Fig. 10a

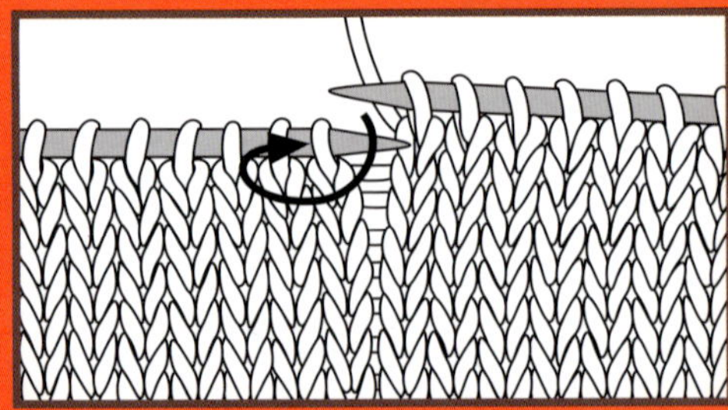

Fig. 10b

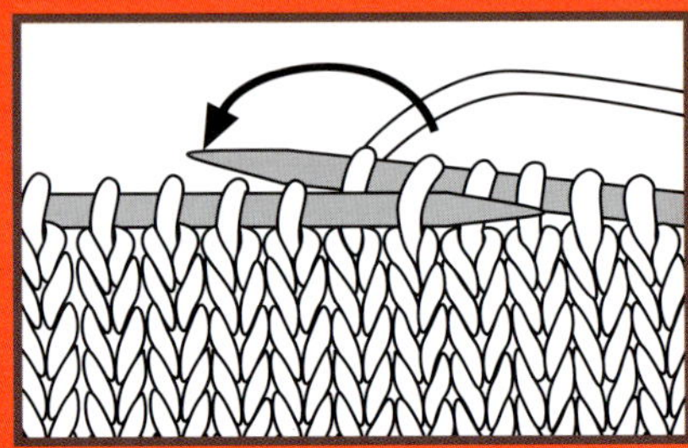

Fig. 11

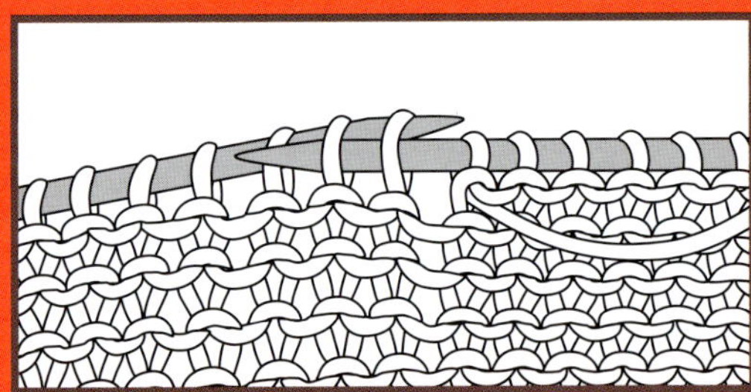

RIGHT TWIST
(abbreviated RT)

Knit into the **front** of the second stitch on the left needle ***(Fig. 12a)***, then **knit** the first stitch ***(Fig. 12b)***, letting both stitches drop off the needle at the same time.

Fig. 12a

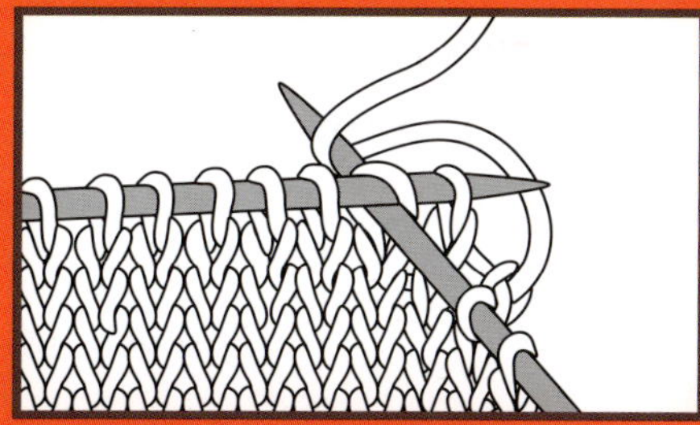

Fig. 12b

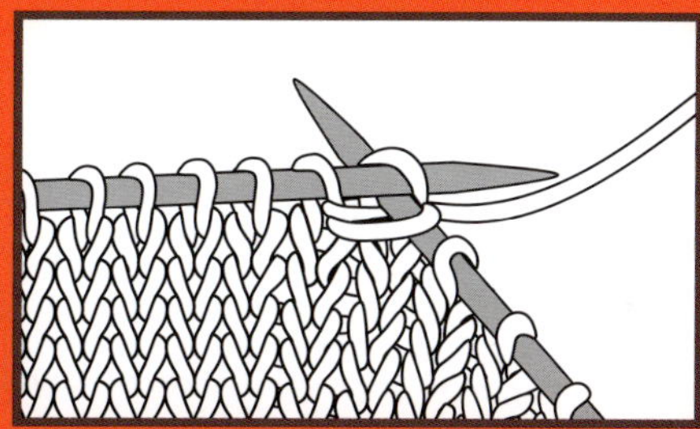

LEFT TWIST *(abbreviated LT)*

Knit into the **back** of the second stitch on left needle ***(Fig. 13a)***, then **knit** the first stitch ***(Fig. 13b)***, letting both stitches drop off the needle at the same time.

Fig. 13a

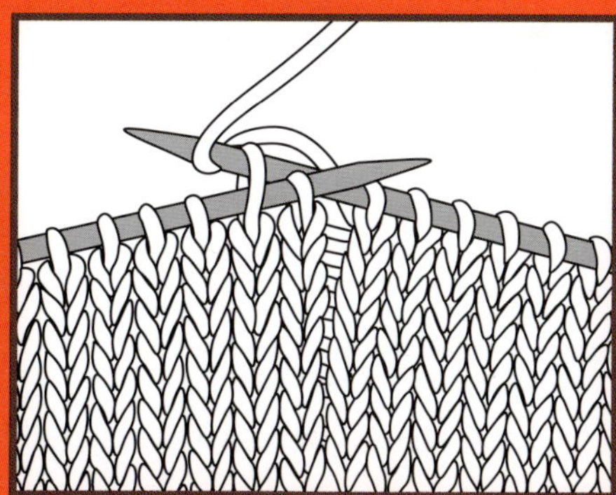

Fig. 13b

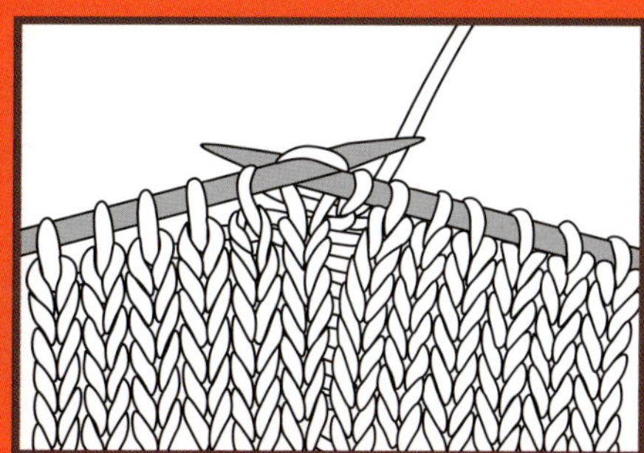

PICKING UP STITCHES

When instructed to pick up stitches, insert the needle from the **front** to the **back** under two strands at the edge of the worked piece ***(Figs. 14a & b)***. Put the yarn around the needle as if to **knit**, then bring the needle with the yarn back through the stitch to the right side, resulting in a stitch on the needle.

Repeat this along the edge, picking up the required number of stitches.

A crochet hook may be helpful to pull yarn through.

Fig. 14a

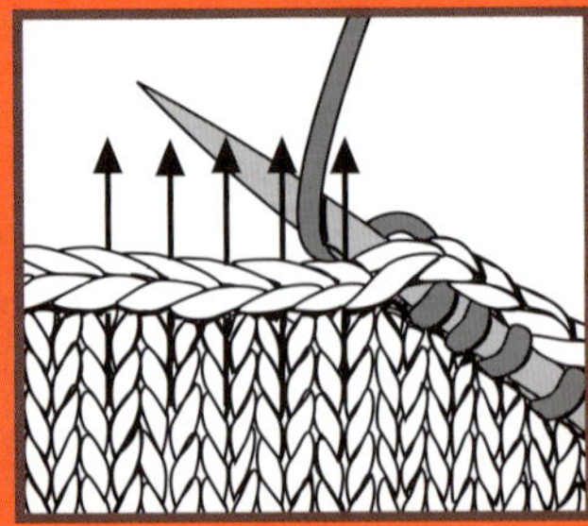

Fig. 14b

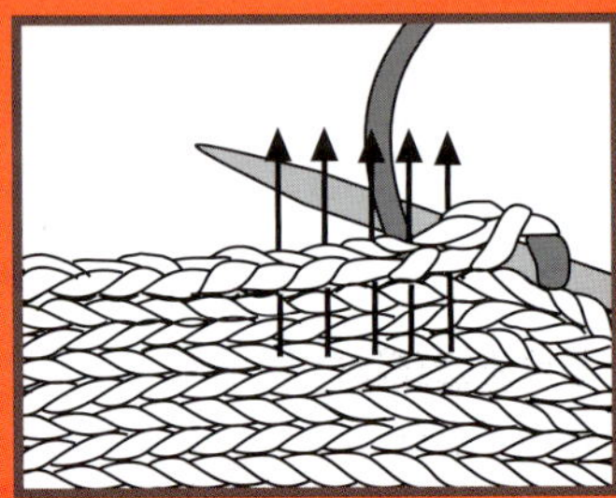

WEAVING SEAMS

With the **right** side of both pieces facing you and edges even, sew through both sides once to secure the seam. Insert the needle under the bar **between** the first and second stitches on the row and pull the yarn through ***(Fig. 15)***. Insert the needle under the next bar on the second side. Repeat from side to side, being careful to match rows. If the edges are different lengths, it may be necessary to insert the needle under two bars at one edge.

Fig. 15

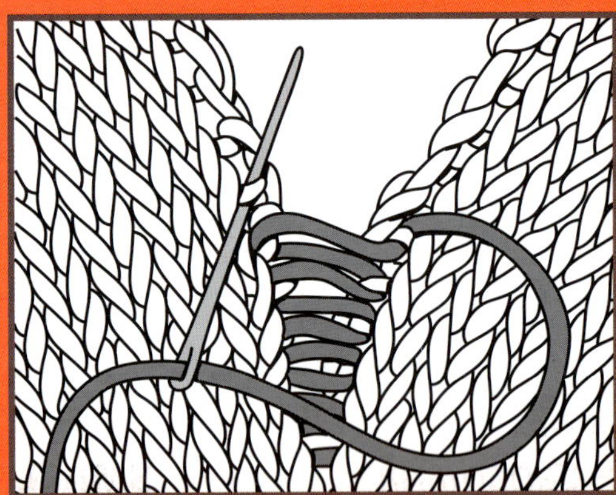

3-NEEDLE BIND OFF

Holding pieces with **right** sides together and needles parallel to each other, insert a third needle as if to **knit** into the first stitch on the front needle and into the first stitch on the back needle ***(Fig. 16)***. Knit these two stitches together and slip them off the needle. ★ Knit the next stitch on each needle together and slip them off the needle. To bind off, insert the left needle into the first stitch on the right needle and pull the first stitch over the second stitch and off the right needle; repeat from ★ across until all of the stitches on the front needle have been bound off.

Fig. 16

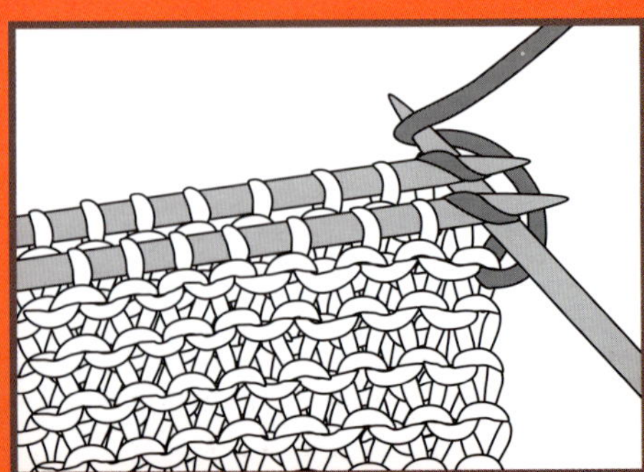